Aspen Out Of Bounds

"My Crazy life in Aspen during
the late sixties and seventies,
its aura of wild hedonism, drugs,
rock and roll, my crazier friends
and famous people."

Charles K. Spetz

DEDICATION

Dedicated to Paul D. McCarthy,
McCarthy Creative Services, whose editing
excellence and patience were so valuable to this
story, and to those of us who got so far out of
bounds they never came back in.

ASPEN OUT OF BOUNDS

Copyright © 2007 by Charles K. Spetz

All Rights Reserved

ISBN-10: 0-979-0999-5-1

ISBN-13: 978-0-9790999-5-3

For Orders or Info

Contact: AOOB

PO Box 82439

Portland, OR 97282

Email: aspenoutofbounds@yahoo.com

Printed in the USA by Printmedia Books

www.printmediabooks.com

TABLE OF CONTENTS

PROLOGUE

In the fall of 1964, when I enrolled at Kent State University, was when I really got started up. I was eighteen years old and this was the first time in my life I was living on my own and started running pretty wild, spending a couple of years in college, joining a top fraternity, spending a summer tending bar in Lake George NY, then leaving school to play piano (which I'd done since age 8) with a rock band. I traveled and played in NY,DC, then back in Ohio and off to Chicago in time for the 68 Democratic Convention and attendant riots, then on to Aspen Colo, where most of this story takes place. And these were crazy intense times, after our president was assassinated, then the Viet Nam war, the revolutionary counter culture, the whole world seemed to have been turned upside down and everyone was looking for something, me included. Not that any of us really knew what we were looking for, as the traditional values were challenged and many accepted stereotypes were seen to be errant, though in many instances there was nothing solid to replace the old views. Aspen in the late sixties and seventies was like a new frontier, with a mixture of influences and old, a beautiful big wild small place with seemingly endless possibilities, people moving through from all parts of the world, some to stay, others just travelers. A free spirited place of serious partying and playing, full of new substances and new attitudes, a hot spot of a mixing kettle.

This story is decidedly pre-Virtual Reality, not that we didn't fuck around with our own alternative states of Being in the Aspen of the early seventies. Let it snow, let it snow, let it snow. To the naked, Middle-American eye, we may have looked like run-of-the mill hippie ski-bums. But while the straight world slaved away in its white-collar rat-race and manicured its *Leave It To Beaver* lawns, we were the ones who had everything -- the best skiing, drugs, women, food, wine, cars, planes, boats. Think *Dynasty* on drugs, or Woodstock on skis, swathed in the cannabis-scented hedonism of an era.

This is not a story about Twelve-Stepping your way into natural nirvana. No stints at Betty Ford, no high-drama, glamour-grunge recantations of the Tao of Dope in favor of the virtuous path of Christ Jay-sus Lord A-mighty. Make no mistake;

drugs were a major part of those glory days; they made wild times wilder, the orgasm of Pure Play exhilarating beyond words. In real life, and especially in my life in Aspen, not all stories have a moral. And not all scams break down neatly into White Hats versus Black Hats. I guess you could say I was a guy who wore a lot of hats.

Gotta pay to play, though. Money to burn could lead to crash-and-burn. There was a phenomenal rate of attrition, for sure. We died from avalanches, plane crashes, motorcycle and car wrecks, drug overdoses, bullets and bombs. Some of us fried our brains on psychedelics; others wound up trading Rocky Mountain paradise for long, purgatorial stints in steel-gray penitentiaries. Casualties were mourned but not moralized. Shit happens. Instant Karma. Don't let your consequences fuck around with my truth. And have a nice day, dude.

Our shamans were the likes of Jack Kerouac, Bob Dylan, Tim Leary, the Beatles and Stones; our Meccas Kent State, Antioch, San Francisco, New York, Chicago and Aspen and later Miami and Beverly Hills. It was obvious to my generation we'd been lied to about recreational drugs, with the dangers of pot and acid falsely equated with junk and speed. And after our president was assassinated by persons obviously other than Lee Harvey Oswald and the evidence locked up for 75 years, many of us were skeptical of the official government line from the get-go. It seemed to us that the last thing the tobacco and liquor industries wanted was another range of pleasure products to compete with their often more harmful addictive substances. We were part-outlaws, like old-fashioned, glamorous bootleggers, and part-neo-capitalist pioneers.

We saw ourselves, then, as well-intentioned, more-or-less virtuous Americans who were simply not buying into a scam, our appetites and needs contrary to the offerings of Establishment death-peddlers.

I decided to write about this part of my life in Aspen from 68-78 because this period best reflected what the complexities of my life were. It was all there in the "undiscovered Aspen" to discover and learn from, the town like the mountains, with a soft beautiful cover of pure white snow, but just underneath a brutal sharp edge of rock.

So this story of my ten years in Aspen is kind of raw and wild like the times, with lots of questions and not enough answers. There were many fantastic wonderful experiences, but also many choices and happenings that weren't so nice. The good parts were probably as good as any of us have ever been fortunate enough to have, and I'm certainly not proud of and real embarrassed by some of the bad ones. One thing that was true about these times is that we were usually somehow, some way, way out of bounds.

Please enjoy
our trip.

Chales K. Spetz
Portland, OR
Jan. 2007

"Some names were changed"

CHAPTER 1:

Chicago "Rock Star"
to Aspen "Hippie Ski Bum"

It was a couple of days after Christmas, 1967, I was 21 years old and had just traveled about twelve hours in a 1950 Chevy panel truck driven by my best high school buddy's older brother Felix along with all the amps, musical equipment and members of our rock band that I was playing keyboards with. We slogged through snowstorms and general bad driving conditions from Dayton, Ohio to Chicago where we had a booking at a big nightclub, and where we were sure the big-time awaited. The trip was exhausting and when we finally pulled up in front of Barnaby's on State Street it was about 10:30 at night and we were a mess. The owner, Big Phil, was real glad to see us and just said "Glad you made it, you're just in time, go get set up, you're on next, knock 'em out". We couldn't believe it, I mean we were already pretty well shot, road weary, dingy, punchy, rest-deprived, burned-out, and more and now we had to not only carry our gear up a narrow steep stairway to the elevated stage, but then also perform. We were here and this was our shot, so lets get at it. Somehow, maybe because we were so loose, we managed three sets that night, finishing up at 4:30 am, with every set and song receiving boisterous cheers and ovations which helped keep us going. We finally fell into a hotel and slept for a day and when we returned to the club the next night we learned that we would be the house band there for a while, trading sets with many other groups, including the likes of CTA (later to become Chicago), REO Speedwagon, Little Richard, and others. This was our bread and butter for most of that winter of 68 with occasional gigs at other clubs, such as The Store, Store Annex, Rush up, Rushover, Mr. Kelly's, Mother Blues in Old Town, and others. We performed under the name Rush, chosen for a number of reasons, among them the way we arrived in the city, and the fact that Rush Street was the area where we did our thing. That spring in March and April, we went on the road out to suburban areas of Chicago and also a kind of college circuit that included clubs like DJ's in Madison, Wi, and Grandmother's in East Lansing, Mi. These were fun, fairly well paying gigs, and we made some good friends with the local musicians we worked with there. Then back home to Chicago where Aaron Russo was opening a major club called the Electric Theater where we were to be the house band starting in June, opening for major acts such as The Who and Velvet Underground. This place was a large, cavernous converted warehouse, its main hall built in a circle with floor to forty-foot-high ceilings of solid white wall, kind of like being inside a huge bowl or soup can. Suspended from the ceiling in the center was a light and sound control pod, from which a bank of projectors put out a 360 degree light show on the walls. An acid trip without the chemical or the threat of the law, though that didn't stop many of us from doubling our pleasure. This room was immense, holding several thousand people, and with the wall of sound from hundreds of Marshall amps and the surrounding of the 360 floor-to-ceiling projected light show, the whole effect could be quite disorienting. The local ordinances in Chicago had the clubs open until 5 a.m. so the bands didn't finish performing until around 4:30. We would then proceed to the local all-night pancake house with our crew and the night's catch of groupies, friends, hangers-on, etc. Our city life was hotels, rehearsals, gigs, crowds, setting up and tearing down, parties, studios and a fairly constant buzz. Life was good. We were locally somewhat famous (or at least known), which scored us primadonna type hero treatment all over town. It was a good time to be a "rock'n'roll star," if only on a small scale. Of course, we didn't see it that way. We were always just one phone call away, we deemed, from the right A&R man at Warners or Capitol or Columbia, and a fat record deal, a national tour, and the superstar status of the Beatles, Stones, and Who all rolled into one hard-driving Midwestern band.

The thing about Chicago then was the buzz which was there when we arrived and just kept getting louder. There was an electricity in the air that was almost palpable. Not the acid-blown Flower Power of San Francisco or the decadent cooler-than-thou New York Warhol scene, but a crazed urban vitality in which the madness of the Sixties fused with good old Heartland optimism and industriousness. We were settled into a pretty regular routine, playing gigs four or five times a week, usually at two different locations. Hence setups and teardowns, sound-checks and all, a substantial set of logistics for a gang not always ready for the grind of a schedule. We also had drugs and groupies to do, two tasks of at least equal importance to making music. After our last set we would usually go in a group to an all-night restaurant, sometimes Mammy's pancake house on Rush St., right behind the Delaware Towers where we lived. There might be fifteen or twenty people in our party, with the night pairings to be decided among several qualified volunteers. The rock'n'roller had truly replaced the four-letter jock as the object of teenage female libido, and we were loving it. Aspiring rock stars strove not so much to be Mick Jagger as to screw all the chicks he did. We had our own versions of small-time Marianne Faithfulls and Anita Pallenbergs, not as storied but just as hippie-chick-sexy and willing. Buy a babe a plate of dollar-pancakes, then take her back to the hotel for the bump, an attempt to be functional by two or three the next afternoon. Afternoons would be either rehearsals, equipment packing or moving, sometimes recording or photo shoots, or just staying caught up on enough essentials to have a semi-normal life. Even minor rock stars had bills to pay and hangovers to treat with Alka-Seltzer and massive doses of Vitamin C. It was a fast pace, with dizzying possibilities, yet our feeling that things were going to work out persisted and we kept our eyes on the prize. I've always liked that expression; shit, was it Ali's or Martin Luther King's? You can see that the zealous political idealism of the times pretty much escaped me. But from the slogans and the passionate activism I did manage to absorb, by osmosis, a kind of stubborn optimism, not always with grounds. But an optimism all the same. While I maintained a general optimism, by now in August, when I thought about my musical performance I started to lose this optimism as I realized I was not playing very well, not growing as an artist at all.

I had started piano lessons when I was eight years old, studying classical, theory, pop, and then some jazz. I did the talent show thing, playing always some standard difficult piece, such as Malaguena, Slaughter on 10th Avenue, Bumble Boogie, Maple Leaf Rag, that type of material. Then for a time, I would do these dinner gigs, like for the Lyons Club or the Kiwanas club, where I would play one or two pieces, get a check for 50 or sometimes 100 bucks, have a nice dinner and do a little hobnobbing with the pillars of the community. Some pretty sweet little action when you're a twelve year old kid trying to hustle paper routes for your main spending money. By the eighth grade, I was playing as the accompanist for a couple of string quartets, then got together a little group with a bass, electric guitar and a drummer and started playing the school dances. I guess I had been a quick learner, and was blessed with some musical genes, as my mother could sit at the piano and play any song she heard perfectly, though she couldn't read a note of music. And I had pretty big hands and good coordination, so the piano was sort of natural for me. When I smashed the first two fingers on my right hand working at the local gas station and they didn't heal right, I had another surgery so they would fit between the black keys and I could still play.

Then when I left Kent State, it was to go on the road playing electric piano for a blues band. When that broke up, back home to Dayton, where I jumped into a local bar and road band, playing a little Farfisa electric organ. While staying back at the family home for awhile and rehearsing the new group, my mother took exception to my smoking material which she found and decided that the local cops would be able to sort out the problem. And even though I had been very close with my dad since I was little and he worked nights and so spent lots of afternoon time with me playing chess and cards, I couldn't believe my own family would get me busted so I left home now for real, and would remain out of touch with them for years.

This was most of the group that I now found myself with here in Chicago, where I used a Hammond B3 and two 122 Leslies and a Wurlitzer electric piano on top of the B3 blowing through two Fender Super Reverb amps. At 22 years old now, I had all the gear, the chicks, the costumes, the life style of an almost top hippie rock star. I'm just a shade under six feet tall, always lean and wiry, with blond hair and blue eyes and real young looking, and since grade school have always had lots of girlfriends around. With all this shit I did have together, the one thing that I didn't have together enough to suit me was my chops. I mean, where throughout all my performing as a kid, I had always practiced religiously, and sounded like it. People always told me that I was hot. But now, in the thick of the scene, I had not practiced, was not using my potential, was just playing at a level that was barely adequate. Whether as a result of some kind of aftershock from all the LSD I had done at Kent(when the stuff was still legal, and being studied by the Psych department, hence carrying some high brow approval) or what, I wasn't sure, but the fact was I was playing like shit, just kind of faking it, while the players in the other bands we traded sets with were all sounding very hot, making matters even worse for my head.

This began to eat at me, because I knew that I had the ability to bring my playing up to an acceptable level. I wasn't so different from the overachieving Honors student I'd been only a few years before; hedonism was my religious calling, but my practical German/Swedish heritage chided me for settling for professional mediocrity. I thought the solution then was for me to hire a keyboardist to take my place and focus on the business aspects while I took some time to school myself again and get in the woodshed. I realize that this seems like a roundabout fix rather than a cure, but at the time it seemed to make sense. I just could not handle myself going through the motions and not really saying anything musically any longer. I knew I could do better, but I didn't know how to change without stepping away from it for a while. And by finding a replacement for myself, and moving (I thought) into the management end there would still be no stopping me. I did have mixed feelings of course, and it was tough to think about taking myself offstage, this wasn't a real well thought out move, I was just deciding something in a hurry and going with it, just taking action and hoping for the best.

I called back home to Dayton and found Ray Bushbaum, a kid I had grown up with, who had always been a real talented natural piano player. I had always thought Ray was a better rocker than me, and he had played with several top local bands, but my call caught him between gigs so he agreed to pack up and head to the Windy City to take the job with my group. Then in September, I made a deal with our band's managers to head back to Ohio and Michigan to sign up some other acts for the management company we had formed. In the previous August of that summer of 1968 while back gigging at Barnaby's on State Street, we had done some shopping at the little boutiques that were all up and down the street, just a few doors from the club. They sold the funky shiny hip, hip bell bottoms, flowered and ruffled shirts, posters, papers, all the stuff you needed to look hot onstage. And the salesgirls were all hot, young chicks trying to score a musician. Well, as my trousers were being fitted, and my outfits coordinated I was targeted by one named Sparrow, who though only 19, was one of the managers of the shop. She was very self assured, cute with waist length dark hair, blue eyes and big tits, so being any kind of her object did not pose a problem for me. And when I told her of my pending change and road trip, she jumped right in with her 66 Mustang convertible, held me tight and we were off. Even though I had had lots of girlfriends by then, this was the first time I had actually lived with a girl for more than a night or two, and here we went, cruising together as a couple, on the road. From an act of convenience for a business trip, now I was caught, which didn't sink in right away with me, but I'm sure this was the main part of her plan the whole time. Anyway, we rolled back to Kent and signed up a great act, Marblecake, an R&B group with a black male-and-female front duo, nice Ohio people with a lot of talent and big potential. Also while in Kent, we got together with my friend, Joe Walsh, who had grown up nearby and was a very talented natural musician, and had a college band called

"The Measles", who were pretty amazing. Joe had taken over from Glen Schwartz a Cleveland band, The James Gang, and wanted me to join him and play piano for the group. Instead, I wanted him to bring the group to Chicago where my new partners and I could be their managers and arrange a recording deal. In a brilliant business career move on my part (right), we did neither and Sparrow and I were on our way down the road, out of town.

Then in Michigan, where my band had played several clubs and made many musician friends and contacts, I recruited Plain Brown Wrapper, a versatile group of music majors who all sang and played multiple instruments. These guys were great people too—smart, professional, devoid of arid music school pretensions. I returned to Chicago at the end of September with a sense of accomplishment and renewed confidence. Maybe this was the beginning of a new career as rock talent scout and promoter. I could be Brian Epstein without the neuroses. A fleeting daydream, but again, back then everything seemed possible.

Then came the now-infamous Democratic Convention end of August 1968 along with all the

crass cynical establishment brutality that our
hippie lovey-dovey generation was so firmly allied
against. On Thursday in the park, during the
convention at a demonstration, several of us had
to bail off a 15 foot high embankment to avoid
getting our heads bashed for no good reason by a
gang of baton-wielding overfed Chicago cops. This
was after being warned the previous week by the
bagman Sergeant at Barnaby's to stay off the
street for the next two weeks. The cops knew in
advance what was going to transpire; the whole
riot thing was not even close to a spontaneous
occurrence. In the midst of what had been a
happening, loose, easy town we now had martial
law, out-of-control cops bashing nonviolent people,
the whole city gripped by a meanness too strong
to make sense. Not anarchy; that somehow
implies a fair fight.

And with the National Guard patrolling the
streets in front of the closed-up nightclub, there
we all were in the next-door loft, two bands set up,
most of the club owners, lots of groupies and bar
help, rocking on at full volume. A 1968 take on
the Titanic orchestra playing away while the ship
was sinking. The bands were surrounded by kegs
of beer on tap, cases of wine, feasts of food, and a

pile of weed on a spread-out newspaper on a table. Musicians from several bands took turns jamming, as did a couple of National Guard guys who had managed to sneak away from their sergeants. Kind of like Vietnam in a microcosm; the soldiers were pawns as much as the civs.

With the riots and violent confrontations raging outside, the party still lasted a day and a half. At the end of the revelry, one of my pals, Reno, the black drummer for Baby Huey (the 12-19 piece black soul act that was the number one band in Chicago), told me he needed help with a "mission." I agreed, since something like that usually ended with scoring contraband goodies. Thus it was that Reno had me driving Sparrow's '66 Mustang downtown at about nine o'clock at night to "give some dude a ride." Sounded innocuous enough. We pulled in front of a local TV station and this wild-haired guy came sprinting out and leaped into the car. "Book it," Reno said, and I floored the Mustang. Both he and the newcomer were laughing. Gasping, Reno introduced me to our passenger: Abbie Hoffman, who had been commandeering the TV studio for political reasons, of course. Though Reno had worked me a little, the cause was righteous, so I was glad to do my small part for the revolution.

After all this and after dealing with the big city thing for a couple months Ray was burned out, or maybe just homesick for the small town Ohio scene, whatever, he was gone, and I was playing again, though I hadn't done any practicing and still was uncomfortable with my act. Then one night maybe a week or so after the convention, we had just finished a set at Barnabys, and were out front in the parking lot taking a break, most of the band, some bar patrons and help, just kind of cooling off, having a smoke, getting ready for our last set. Across the street, on the sidewalk in front of Your Father's Moustache, a famous major restaurant, there are two guys talking. Then they seem to be arguing, with voices raised and suddenly one of them yells "Fuck me, fuck you", pulls out a pistol, sticks it in the other guys ear and fires. Just like that. I can't believe my eyes as the victim drops like a bag of sand and the shooter just walks down the street, gets on a bus and is out of there. This was about thirty feet from where I'm sitting on a little wall and I'm freaked out. Gritty city. Then its time to go back inside and get up onstage and play music. I was in some kind of shock, to say the least. No peace and love here tonight. This was just too much, maybe one of those last straw things.

Somehow, I can't remember how, I had run into one of my fraternity brothers from Kent, Rick Hedford, who had a business degree and was living in Chicago working a nine to five suit job. He started hanging out with the band and was kind of part of our support team.

Besides Sparrow, I had several other on and off girlfriends and it was getting confusing trying to figure out who I was supposed to be sleeping with when. Then one of them, Jean, announced that she was pregnant and it was mine. I'm still only 22 years old and not even really an adult myself, so could no way imaging myself in parenthood. Plus, I had heard stories forever about chicks who claimed to be pregnant to catch their guy, or ones who were not even pregnant but claimed to be for the same purpose. Besides, we had only been together a couple of times and although she was a beautiful lovely girl, I couldn't really make myself believe it was all true.

When brother Hedford announced that he had rented a mobile home outside a place named Aspen in Colorado and was packing up and getting out of the city, I didn't need much persuading to join him. Since Sparrow had a pretty good car, the Mustang convertible, and was ready to do anything to get me away from the other girls, we had a team and with a U-Haul trailer full of stuff, were ready for the long journey, we thought.

My band was in disarray, I had been too close to too much violence, I had girls chasing me with pregnant claims, so I guess I was pretty confused. There were too many issues happening at once for me to be able to deal with, or maybe that is just rationalization, I'm not sure. I wasn't very tough, wasn't very savvy, just a naïve kid from Ohio who wanted to be some kind of star, without knowing what was really going on. My youthful idealism had taken a few hard hits, and I was more confused than angry or resentful, and after living through Kennedy's assassination, the Democratic convention and the Vietnam fiasco I was developing a strong cynicism and distrust of the law and authorities. Everything in Chicago just seemed to be closing in on me and I guess I was ready for an escape. So we packed up the car and trailer and drove. And drove. And drove until we hit the continental divide and a blizzard and had to stay overnight at a small cabin motel in Loveland, Colo, because the road over the pass was

closed by the snow. Finally the road opened and
we could go the last six or seven hours and pulled
into the breathtaking Roaring Fork Valley. This
was an escape from what I sort of knew, but into
what I had no idea.

You think you're a star
but you're not up to par
so leave the bar
and go get in the car
go rolling down the tar
go way afar
till you don't even
know where you are

CHAPTER 2:

Life on the Bad Boys Ranch

It was the first week of November 1968 as we finally pulled into the Gerbaz Mobile Village eight miles down-valley from Aspen in the Roaring Fork Valley. We were pretty burned-out from a grueling cross country drive and checked into our three bedroom two bath mobile home and crashed out. After a good twelve hour rest we got up and I got my first look in the daylight at where we had traveled to. Going outside it seemed like all I could see was sky, more deep blue sky than I had ever seen or even imagined. Big sky, lots of sky, you could just see for miles and miles in all directions. And what I thought were the mountains but were really just hills were snow covered and took off upward all around us. Since we were well over a mile high in elevation the air was dry and cold, and very thin. It seemed to take a while to catch my breath. First order of business was unpacking the U-Haul and turning it in down the road at Glenwood Springs, past the burgs of Basalt, Emma, and Carbondale, where the road (rt 82) takes off from I70 and heads south 40 miles to Aspen. Glenwood Springs was a sleepy kind of cowboy town, Doc Holliday's final resting place, and while boasting the country's largest hot mineral swimming pool, it served as the closest thing to a city for shopping for the whole valley, complete with supermarkets, mercantiles, car dealers, a bowling alley, but still very small town, with a western cowboy feel. After dropping the trailer we headed back up valley and it was time for our first forage into Aspen itself. This was a whole different thing. Where Glenwood Springs still looked like part of middle America, going into Aspen was like going into a different world. Situated at the base of Aspen Mountain, an 11,200 foot monster, at an elevation of 7900 feet the little old mining town was a jewel. Main Street was the only paved road, there were no traffic lights, no neon signs and the town looked to be made up of old Victorian houses, a few stores and shops, one gas station, some old brick commercial buildings, the old opera house, and lots of shacks, shanties, barns and some chalets and A-frames. There were an abundance of motels, restaurants and right in the center of town on main street the historic Hotel Jerome, a three story square building taking up a half-block. The town looked to me like a work in progress, which it was, combining old structures ready for the bulldozer with old ones being restored, and new lodges and buildings going up all over. It seemed like everyone was driving a pickup with a broom and a dog in the back. The people looked like a mix of cowboys, hippies and Europeans, with some crazy looking combinations of all three. No city slickers or preppies seemed to be here. To even get to town from Gerbaz, you had to go uphill past the Snowmass turnoff, negotiate the treacherous Shale Bluffs, a narrow s-turn with cliffs up the south side and a 500 foot sheer dropoff off to the north without any guardrails, then on uphill past Buttermilk mountain (the beginner hill that looked massive to me) finally past the sidehill Aspen Highlands and into town. A lot different than running down Lakeshore Drive in Chicago to get to the nightclubs.

This first trip to town was really to me like going into a new world, lots of culture shock. I didn't know what I would do here, how I would fit in, but I told myself that as beautiful and exotic as the place was I would find some way to be able to stay and make it, finding some type of employment and an income. I remembered that

some of the people I worked with in the bars in
Lake George, NY where I went with some of my
fraternity brothers during summers away from
Kent, had talked of wintering in Aspen and I soon
found Danny Wardwell, who was managing the
bar and nightclub in the Hotel Jerome. It took
some cajoling but I finally talked him into letting
me work the service bar at the nightclub, where
Dudley Moore and the Nitty Gritty Dirt Band
performed. So I had a start in town, modest
though it may have been. And Sparrow got herself
hired as a salesgirl at Carl's Pharmacy, a
combination of drugstore, hardware and sporting
goods outlet along with a small convenience store
type of grocery section. And Hedford, who was a
pretty good handyman, got hired on doing tile
work at the new Aspen Square condominium
project in the middle of town, for good wages. It
looked like we all had a foot in the door and a
chance to become "locals" as the people I worked
with told me was what we full-time residents were
called, as opposed to the tourists who were
referred to as "turkeys". After only one week in
Colorado, before I had a chance to gain any
comfort with my situation, though, I learned
Sparrow and I would need to find other living

accommodations at the insistence of one Joe Day, the redneck Bible thumping mobile home park manager who could not tolerate our unmarried living in sin status. Just what I needed now, stranger in a strange land trying to find a place to live as the town was filled up waiting for the high season to start on Thanksgiving in a couple of weeks. I felt lost and somewhat helpless all over again, along with a good amount of pissed off at the retro asshole. Here I was already willing to make a change from being onstage in front of thousands of people to just a low level member of the work force, and even this big step down was being made difficult. This didn't make much sense, and I was pretty shaken, here goes another rug out from under me. But luck was with us, because one night at the trailer park while using the Laundromat, I had struck up a conversation with two other guys who were also doing laundry. They had been locals for a while, so they were full of good information about the scene. And Steve was a skier, so when I asked him about that, he said he could help us there. But when Karl and Steve mentioned the names of the local bad actors, Limpy and Bud, I got a little excited. "These guys aren't from New York, are they?" I asked, not really expecting to run across in Aspen the bad boys whom I had partied with in Lake George.

"These guys are tough, man. They get high and start fights and always have the police telling them to stay out of town," Karl replied. "Real shitkickers." This sounded like an accurate description of my buddies from Lake George, so I asked where I might find them. I was told they had a ranch right down the road but that it was too dangerous to just show up there: "You just might get your ass shot at or something." But I wasn't put off. I finally convinced Karl and Steve that Limp and Bud were old pals I hadn't seen for some time and that they would be glad to see me.

After twisting a few for the ride, we decided to head on out to the ranch. It was after the dinner hour when we showed up, probably about 8:30 or 9:00. The house looked dark, almost abandoned, and I sensed a good deal – hell, a shitload -- of apprehension from my new friends. We pulled up to the porch and I got out and knocked and started yelling. "Limpy, you sonofabitch, get on out here so somebody can kick your ass!" Karl and Steve were just about pissing their pants, almost certain that somebody would soon open fire and we would all be history.

After a few minutes, Limpy hobbled out (he'd been shot in one leg some years before) to investigate the racket. Of course, he was carrying a revolver, a gigantic hunting knife and an attitude. "Okay, where's the big mouth who's gonna kick my ass!" he bellowed.

"That would be me, dickwad," I announced as I stepped into the light.

Glancing around, Limpy looked ready to shout or shoot, but then he saw me. He got a confused look on his face as he struggled to make gray matter functional. Eventually the old memory bank kicked in and he realized why I looked vaguely familiar. "Chuckles, you asshole, you are the worst!" he laughed. "What the fuck are you doing here? Get your ass inside and have some dinner and drinks, you old sumbitch!" Needless to say, Karl and Steve were greatly relieved at not having to make a high-speed escape out of there dodging projectiles.

It is only fair to both Karl and Steve to point out that their apprehension was less a reflection of their lack of courage than a demonstration of their common sense.

Soon we were partying in the living room at the ranch, Karl, Steve, myself with Limpy, Bud,

Nutty Ned, a local friend, and Rivers, a ranch resident from Lake George, eating, drinking, throwing knives, just generally getting a good buzz. Eventually I described my situation as a future evictee, bummed that after moving my life and my old lady's to Aspen we were going to be out on the street. When Limpy heard this he immediately offered refuge. "If you still want to call me a friend and don't want your ass kicked, I'll rent you a bedroom for eighty bucks a month." The old ranch house had six or seven bedrooms, and the one he was offering was vacant due to an unscheduled vacation courtesy of the county for its previous occupant.

My new living accommodations thus settled and all the beer at the house drained dry, it was time to head into town to do some serious celebrating. As this was still a few days before Thanksgiving and still the off-season there were only two bars open, the Pub and Galena St. East. The usual route was first to the Pub to have a couple quick ones, give Kendall, the owner, some shit. Next was Galena St. a block away, a dark, stone-walled basement with loud live music, hot women and all sorts of drunken and drug-fueled craziness. In other words, my kind of place.

We lasted about fifteen-twenty minutes at the Pub before suddenly all the other people, tables, chairs and drinks ended up in a nervous grouping at one end of the room, while our group occupied the rest of the bar. At our table Limpy was holding court, though his insults were directed mainly at us; nobody was pissed, but I guess we were all hooting and cussing and otherwise not exactly behaving like perfect little gentlemen. We sort of noticed we were being ostracized by the other patrons, but at the time this arrangement seemed reasonable to us. That is, until Kendall decided to call the cops. We decided to shift the impromptu party to Galena St. After not seeing me for a while, Limpy and Bud were, I think, inclined to flex and show off a little. They were doing a good job of it too.

Galena St. was rocking and I mistakenly figured that somehow we would be absorbed in the scene and therefore have an anonymous good time. Wrong. It took less than a half hour for Rivers to suckerpunch one of the bartenders over the countertop. This was the only excuse necessary for most of the crowd to start brawling. So here in my first night on the Aspen bar scene, my long-lost pals had managed to close the only two bars in town that were open. The final pathetic picture had the lead town police officer at the bottom of the steps begging Bud to just please go home because nobody wanted any more trouble. Bud let him sweat it out for several agonizing minutes before he finally relented and gave the cop a break.

The following day Sparrow and I took up residence at   Limp's ranch. It was less commune than hippie rooming house. No group hugs, no mantra-chanting. And you hit on somebody else's woman at your own risk. Along with Limpy and his old lady White, the residents were Bud (a stocky, scrappy Irishman with a great sense of humor and a love of brawling to equal Limpy's), Rivers (another of the Lake George hellraisers), his wife Martha, and "Doc" Pen, an introverted alcoholic type also from Lake George who was Limpy's main slave, gofer, whipping boy and general grunt. The source of Pen's devotion to Limpy was apparently unknown, but both seemed content with the Master-Slave dynamic. The rest of us were pretty much equals, but Pen seemed to be Limpy's one-man cult following.

Aside from picking barroom fights, one of Limpy's other accomplishments was his method of hunting elk. He would watch the fields around the ranch house every morning in the fall as the snowfall increased and deepened the pack. Soon would come the day that the herd moved down into the back pasture. Then I'd see Limp take his coffee out to the porch with the 30.06 rifle. He would take his time, sip coffee, find a comfy bench mount out the screened window for the barrel, pick the biggest bull and drop him. Then it was time for Pen to go to work, taking the jeep and a chain out to drag the bull to the barn. There were always plenty of delicious elk steaks at the ranch.

Fortunately we had gotten moved in time for Thanksgiving and the proper traditional observation with the turkey, several potato dishes, gravy, cranberries, a spread of vegetables, greens, breads, biscuits, ham, venison, trout, pumpkin, mince, berry, you know, all the pies. Add a complete bar, wines, beers, joints, all the residents and a few outlaw guests all cleaned up, showered, shaved, wearing Sunday clothes and displaying non-objectionable behavior, all at the same time. Staggers the imagination. All in all a fine quality day with feast and football games on tv, all the girls in the kitchen and us boys just kickin' back feeding the face and shootin' the shit. We had dogs in a pack outside, and lots of dart games, then outside to throw knives and hatchets, snowballs, back in for rations, back out, just a loose well enjoyed holiday. The guests were all people who had been in the valley for a while so talking to them was a good, much needed source of local knowledge.

They explained to me that the town had only a few thousand year-round residents (locals) but beginning on Thanksgiving upwards of 50,000 visitors (tourists or turkeys) would flood the place to ski, eat, drink, party and generally consume at a prodigious rate thereby guaranteeing the livelihood of the locals. And the locals were made up of a combination of both ends of the economic strata, from street type hippies to PHD's who were mutually drawn to the fantastic beauty and laid back lifestyle. So being part of the workforce felt like being a member of some type of club or team and there were strict codes about not taking advantage of other locals, only turkeys were fair game. This resentment of the cash cows was tough to get a handle on but the more I had served and waited on them and observed their attitudes and styles, I could see that the ugly American had come out enough that they had earned their due.

And lots of names were connected to faces, jobs and areas, just lots of useful info, and all too soon I had to change and head in to work a short night shift at the hotel, just kind of worked on automatic, just hardly being able to wait to head back to the big old ranch house for some sleep.

Besides the Thanksgiving party, there was most every day some company dropping by, a diverse group of locals, travelers, adventurers, scoundrels and others. There would be people either just returning from or just leaving for different exotic locations, like South or Central America (it seemed that everyone went to Mexico after the ski season), Europe or Asia. Quite a few guys had completed tours in 'Nam, and they could be a squirrely bunch as we all realize. In 1968 shellshock and post-'Nam heroin habits were not very well understood. The vets just seemed like macho freaks with dead eyes, the antithesis of Lucy's kaleidoscope orbs from the Beatles song.

Amazingly, a more impeccable home was nowhere to be found; the ranch rules were very strict regarding that. White, as he called her, was totally subservient to Limp; he picked on her to the point of verbal abuse. If dinner was not on time or cooked to his liking, he'd call her a lazy whore or tell her she was "more useless than tits on a bull." Or sometimes out of sheer spite, he'd break his own rules and litter the place with empty beer cans, filthy plates, and leftover drug paraphernalia. "Look at all this crap! I ought to kick your ass for the way you keep this goddamn house." As with Pen, I was somewhat surprised that White took so much shit from Limpy, since under other circumstances she seemed possessed of a New England-Yankee toughness that belied her slight stature.

One night in early December our group had just come racing up the quarter-mile driveway at a high rate of speed in a snowstorm, followed at a short distance by a Highway Patrol car. Our Jeep was in the barn and out of sight by the time the H.P. got up to the house. As the officer stopped to look around, out from the kitchen came White in her housecoat carrying a 30.06 deer rifle. "This here is private property and you're not invited, so turn around and get out of here now!" she warned. That was exactly what happened. We never heard anything more from the H.P. or anyone else regarding the incident. One other night, a week or so later, still December, the horses got loose, so after we all returned from town about 1:00 a.m.

we had a mission: to find the horses. At about 5 degrees above zero, for the next several hours White ran us dudes into the ground as she tirelessly caught up to the horses, trapped and roped them, and brought them home. I'm fairly sure that Limpy held the lease, but White seemed to take a pride of ownership in the ranch and especially the horses. She often cantered bareback on her favorite palomino Sugar, and if she got thrown, she'd laugh it off and clamber back on. If she happened to land in horse shit she'd wax this side of philosophical: "Horse-shit's nothing else but recycled hay!" It seemed a useful piece of wisdom; maybe that was how she explained to herself all the crap she got from Limpy.

After being there for 3 or 4 weeks, we fell into a routine with Sparrow doing her thing at Carl's and me working the service bar at the Jerome. We were surviving, but just barely, as my job was just kind of a fringe bartender job, and not steady or lucrative enough to provide real stability. But we were getting in the flow, meeting people and I was starting to learn a little about what kind of place I had ended up in.

I thought, especially with Christmas coming up, that if I could only land a real bartender job I could move up to the next level and become a solid local with some stability, moving upward and onward. This was the next goal, but at the time seemed like it should be easy, since I had learned in Lake George how to be a topnotch bar man, but here in the little mining town it was a closed system, and more important than what you knew was who you knew. And my few friends from New York either couldn't or wouldn't hook me up with the good job, so I was a little frustrated and a lot broke. But life went on and there were great times at the ranch with some spectacular shindigs. This Christmas of 1968 had an old west flavor, with a feast to even surpass the excess of Thanksgiving. We had pit roasted elk, venison, pig, turkey, pheasant, trout, potatoes, vegetables, pies of every type (all fresh baked), fruits, kegs of beer, cases of wine and whiskey, smokables, lickables, dropables and about one hundred of our closest friends. When I dropped Nutty Ned off in town after the Christmas party, I knew I was watching a scene I'd never forget. Ned proceeded to walk down the street, in a duster and a plainsman hat, carrying his meat-cutting knives in one hand, a plastic bag of raw steaks and meat in the other. He was followed by his dog, Sydney, a worldly-wise Australian shepherd ambling easy with a big doggy grin stretching her muzzle. It was a sight to frighten small and large children, and in fact a few of the younger ones abandoned half-formed snowmen and ran back inside their houses.

One night I saw at the Pub, in January, 1969, Ned was trying to get four or five guys to fight him and they weren't going for it. To goad them into fighting he smacked the girl who was with them. Her nose gushed blood and her lip was split open. The guys with her understandably had to retaliate. They used tire irons and chains on Ned and he had scars and welts for a long time, but all the other guys went to the hospital with broken jaws, noses, etc. Nutty Ned is a story unto himself and was one of my favorite people in Aspen. To my old lady he was always a gentleman, even protective. Sometimes when Limpy's language got too raunchy, Ned would tersely remind our host that Sparrow was present and to cool it. To me he was a kick to hang out with and never threatening or even surly. I was probably lucky to have started out knowing Ned as a friend because being on his wrong side could be very dangerous. He was a throwback, rumored to have served time in Illinois for cattle rustling before he came to Colorado. A real outlaw while the rest of us were playing cowboys and Indians. He worked as a woodcutter and his strength was prodigious. He could dead-lift over seven hundred pounds even though he was a lanky 6'5. With some missing teeth that gave him a quirky smile and a mostly silent demeanor, Ned struck some folks as at least physically disconcerting. He was, however, very bright with a dry sense of humor. But when provoked or maybe just in a bad mood, he could be violent and unpredictable. In spite of this occasional brutishness, Ned was pleasant to his friends, almost shy. At all the barbecues at the ranch Ned was the head butcher, as he could clean and gut an elk slicker than a whistle. And Sydney could be counted on to guard the meat, not letting any of the other dogs even get close.

For Sparrow and me life was good at the ranch, with a tranquility most of the time that was surprising, considering the various temperaments of the residents. About the only time there was much noise other than during parties was when Limpy became especially abusive to White, and knocked her down the stairs or shoved her around. Incredibly, she always forgave him; it was almost part of the late-sixties, "old lady" code that chicks baked hash brownies, kept a nice house, and put up with shit from their old men. Navajo jewelry, dresses made from Indian bedspreads, and an occasional shiner. Ladies of the Canyon, Aspen-style. And true to the code, White never left him.

And then there was the skiing. Growing up in southern Ohio, I'd never thought much about skiing. It was never part of our world. Although we had some snow in the winter, it's rather difficult to go skiing on a flat cornfield. But Aspen was an adrenaline junkie's dream. Looking up at some of the best ski mountains in the world, watching people zagging down the hill in wingless flight, I fell in love with the sport at first sight. And, to be honest, I also noticed right off the tight butts of the chicks on the slopes, and how the hot women skiers never seemed to hang out with guys who didn't ski. But I had no idea about how to begin; I didn't know anything about the equipment that was required or the means to obtain any. My newfound friend, Steve, had an easy solution. "Just come with me tomorrow at exactly 12:30," he said, "and we'll get you outfitted. I've got a deal."

So the next day, a clear cold February day,
we went at precisely 12:30 to the Buttermilk
rental shop, where he did have a deal of some kind
with the manager. He picked out some Lange
boots, Head Standard skis and a pair of poles. We
simply fitted up everything, packed up, walked
out, and now I had ski equipment. Unwilling to be
a thief, I asked Steve what was up, and he assured
me that he had traded a bag of weed for
everything, so I didn't have to worry. He gave
me a half-day pass and about 30 minutes later we
were at the top of Buttermilk Mountain. It was a
crystal clear day with dark blue sky, a fantastic
panoramic view, loads of light, dry snow. I was
scared shitless. I didn't have a clue what to do
and as soon as we were off the lift, which was an
ordeal in itself, Steve yelled, "Let's go" and took
off down the hill. The only thing I figured made
sense to do was to point the skis downhill and see
how far I could get before I wiped out. I probably
made it a couple hundred yards before I ate it, and
I mean ate it. I was going maybe 35-40 mph
wavering back and forth with no idea of how to
turn, slow down or stop when I couldn't hold it
anymore. I felt like I'd fallen off a roof, with

skis, poles, goggles, and hat scattered all over the hill. My ski career had begun. The adrenaline thrill was the only thing that made the pain seem somehow like a logical trade-off and I knew I had to become a good skier.

Of the many and varied special activities at the ranch, none held a potential for disaster more than the mounted pub raids, one of which I went on in February. In that part of the country in those years, the handgun law required only that a legally carried pistol had to be visible. This expedition began with a great deal of coffee and additives — acid and whiskey. Then we'd saddled and mounted the horses, strapped on the large bore pistols, and trotted six miles up to town at 7900 feet under a clear sky so rich it was more purple or black than blue. There were no traffic lights or neon signs in town yet and most of the roads were dirt. By the time the horses were tied out front we were ready for the ice-cold beer in the subterranean comfort of the Pub. Of course, upon entering we were ordered to surrender our weapons to the cooler while we drank. And drank. And stank. Then Limpy started to have fun. The problem was that his idea of fun was to single out another patron at the bar and begin picking on him. This loud verbal torture could go on for hours with increasing venom. ("Pussy" might give way to "Fucknut" and then "Fucknut" to still more inventive epithets like "Ass-ugly Scrotumface" or "Mama's Little Cumbag.") Despite his drunken state Limpy could become very clever with the putdowns, challenges and mockery, thereby drawing in an ever-growing audience. If he could entice others into the scene, he would do so with glee. Before long, his unfortunate victim must have felt the whole world was against him or watching or both. This became the entertainment and whether the "pigeon" thought it was funny or disgusting, he was nonetheless sharing center-stage with Limpy. I am convinced that some place in his foggy consciousness, Limpy knew exactly what he was doing. The fact that this session ended up in some kind of physical confrontation seemed to have no meaning to him. After the fight that he may have won or lost, Limpy bought drinks from then on for his newest best buddy, regardless of who was victor or vanquished. Most of the other folks in the bar seemed to feel a pained embarrassment witnessing one of these ordeals, but nobody ever intervened. After all, why interrupt the show, uncomfortable as it might have been?

Some help was required later taking care of the horses, nobody saw his gun again for days, and amazingly enough, no major incidents ever arose from these illogical scenarios. Hippie cowboys playing real ones, but with real bullets in our guns. I figured, the drugs we took must have been pretty good, and a damn good thing, too.

Although I was somewhat in awe of my surroundings, it's hard saying why I never put two and two together and figured out why all the travelers always seemed to be carrying a stash of one high quality recreational product or another, or why the boys at the ranch seemed to have access to goodly amounts of cash. I was probably too busy enjoying the fruits of others' illicit labor to worry much about the supply side. Smoke, and you shall receive more to smoke. I didn't care to analyze it beyond that. But there was something of a local subculture that eked an existence from crosstown vehicle transfers. As clandestine as these activities were and needed to be for people's survival, the locals (the *real* locals) shared this common knowledge and a protectiveness against outsiders even though most had no involvement or interest in the action. So there sprung up many different factions that "worked" together. And then there seemed to be no trouble for any of the locals.

At the ranch, few mundane disputes had to do with dope. The morning in late February when Limpy needed Pen to do some chore or another at about 9:00 started innocently enough until it became obvious that Pen was hopelessly hungover and wasn't about to move. I'm sure he was so unconscious his ears didn't even make his brain register the screaming, threatening, increasingly psyched-out Limpy getting revved up for his morning audience of about seven or eight of us crazies. "That motherfuckin', shit-worthless fleshloaf ain't gonna sleep his ass off on my fuckin' time!" Limpy raved to us, stomping back and forth and occasionally kicking a scuffed boot-toe against a chair he probably imagined was Pen's head. Finally, in a lather, Limpy flashed on a solution. "I know how to get him up," he announced reasonably as he loaded the deer rifle and sent a round crashing through Pen's bedroom door. The rabbitty look on Pen's face as he gingerly peeked into the living room one or two seconds later was priceless. Limp hooted, pleased with himself. "Guess your ass is wide-awake now,

Pen!"

Though Sparrow was sexy, voluptuous, and usually horny, and even though we mostly got along, I couldn't help but be tempted every day by the local lovelies. There were loads of really foxy willing chicks all over the place and you'd have to be crazy or gay or blind not to notice. And being someone's possession was wearing thin on me, to say the least. She was loyal, too loyal, and expected the same from me, I mean she was psychotic about it, and I was beginning to feel a little smothered by it all. And at home on the ranch, Limpy's number 2 and number 3 were not especially secret, he even maybe flaunted this to White, who just stoically did her thing. There was an undertone of friction there even when they weren't outright fighting. It was like always boiling right below the surface, and I felt embarrassed for them, but there was nothing anyone could say, because it wasn't anyone else's business really. So as nice as it was on the ranch, and for all the respect that we were all accorded, it still got to the point where it became unbearable for Sparrow. She said she was sure that one day White would just have taken too much, get fed up and take a gun and blow Limp away. And she didn't want to be around when it happened. I had mixed feelings about the whole scene, and would have just as soon stayed, but somehow Sparrow still had enough hold on me that I agreed we would move somewhere else. This was March 1969 and everything in town was still occupied with waiting lists until Easter, the end of high season. This was absolutely the worst time to try to find housing, but somehow we located a cabin down valley about 27 miles out of town at a place called the Wooden Handle on the Frying Pan River outside of a little place called Basalt. I was really quite torn by this impending move. In town, at work or just hanging out, almost everyday I was getting hit on by chicks, real cute chicks, and this was not easy for me to deal with, to pass up on. Yet every time something seemed like it could happen, either the logistics got in the way, or my guilt did the same. So I was in some kind of state of constant frustration. Part of me was content right where I was at the ranch, no problem chasing many girls in town, and it wasn't so much of a problem for me to look the other way at Limp's carrying on, just mind my own business. I could easily have just stayed there and let Sparrow take off if she had to or whatever. But after what we had been through in such a short time, and after all, it was her Mustang that took us out of Chicago, and because of my genuine good feelings and caring for her that I felt, in the end my loyalty to her won out, and I accepted that we were going to move together again. To her I was the end game, she seemed totally satisfied and claimed no desires for anyone else. For me, though, as much as I cared for her, I still was attracted to other girls, and was used to having lots of them, so I had a measure of inner tension to deal with every day. Her passion was somewhat overwhelming, and whether she was a super actress or her feelings were that strong, this strength ruled over my uncertainty. And though I no way felt ready to marry up and settle down with one woman, I still felt we were a good couple, we got along well on a day to day basis, and about most things she had a good sense of humor and a quick wit, although her dedication to us as a unit was still a little overbearing.

With mixed amounts of sadness and relief we left the ranch and headed down valley. I didn't know how this would play out and thought I'd much rather be heading closer to Aspen than farther away, but I didn't see any options so we packed up and were moving again.

And how much do we muse
about what we could lose
from the path we choose
or do we just cruise
with no cares or blues
forgetting our dues
and running our ruse
just lighting the fuse
becoming tomorrow's news

CHAPTER 3:

Living in Cowboy Land

Though only twenty miles, the simple move "down valley" was as big a step culturally as the move from Chicago to Colorado. Our new home was the old homesteaders square cut log cabin of a property called the Wooden Handle (on the Frying Pan River, get it).

Though only twenty miles, the road down the Roaring Fork River from Aspen to Basalt changed about 1500 feet in elevation, twisting most of the way; two-lane travel or somewhat less could be treacherous. Unlike Aspen, the "down valley" areas did not exactly have the benefit of a major influx of tourist revenue and an international as well as elite ambience. The "short" trips down valley induced a culture shock that sometimes bordered on the surreal, depending on what kind of drugs you were taking. Imagine going from Never-Never Land to whatever your vision is of Buttfuck, Egypt, and you'll probably get the picture. So for the last couple of months of that ski season, February and March, 1969, Sparrow and I would make the long drive into town each morning, work all day and sometimes into the evening, then hook up for the long ride back down valley. Depending on the road conditions, this could be a twelve to sixteen hour day. I was trying to make the best of it all, but it didn't take long for this to get old. I still just had the fringe bar job, and our combined income just barely allowed us to exist, with not much free time for fun stuff. Bad as this seemed, when Easter came and ski season ended, all the bars and restaurants closed up, most of the help that had had good jobs all winter headed to Mexico for a couple months of sun, and the town just kind of rolled up and looked like a ghost town. Shit, now what. The only work in the spring were some scattered construction jobs, and you had to be a tool-carrying qualified carpenter to make any kind of living at this. The only laborer jobs seemed to always be promised to someone's little brother or kid or something and things really got thin. I was definitely having second thoughts about what was going on, and was feeling real unsettled and insecure.

Since there weren't really that many of us young folks in the Basalt area and there was only one grocery store, we all pretty much knew each other if only to say hi to or share a ride up the valley, or burn one or whatever.

The struggle the cowboys down valley had with the so-called hippies was a fact of life. I was told of many incidents of cowboys becoming physically abusive, forcibly inflicting haircuts (the down valley version of tarring and feathering). But sometimes the factions managed to forge an uneasy truce. One day at a party at Chuck and Joan's house (a couple from Denver) at Seven Castles, a bunch of us Aspen types and redneck cowboys were actually getting along, drinking and toking and otherwise carrying on outside by the campfire. All until Darren, a wealthy young Denver friend of the hosts, nastily loaded and even more obnoxious than usual, staggered up and started talking trash with one of the cowboy guests. "Kicked any shit lately, Buffalo Bill?" Darren taunted. "Getting them little dogies along OK, or have you finally graduated to sheep? I hear they're better lays." Just as I was struggling to wrest the gallon jug from Darren's sweaty hand, my good friend Joe Poleski, an ex-Marine from Chicago, walked up and delivered a right fist in full stride. After a sickening crack that echoed like a shot, Darren crumpled as if kicked in the face by a mule. He was out cold. The party resumed as if nothing had happened, except that the rednecks were looking at the hippies with a new respect. Forget the peace, love, and granola shit; we freaks understood the persuasive powers of brute force every bit as much as our cowboy brethren.

Not that the cowboys who kept their noses clean, drug-wise, always had it easier. Joe Poleski, Sparrow and I became good friends with Cowboy Frank, a 'Nam veteran with a bad-ass reputation. One time, Poleski told me, while drinking beers and shooting at cans with some buddies, Frank took offense at one guy's mockery of his marksmanship and pistol-whipped the loudmouth into a bloody though thankfully minor concussion. On another occasion, Joe said, he got pissed at a friend for flirting with the same woman in a saloon and calmly walked to the parking lot where he smashed in the dude's windshield with his bare fist. He was maybe 27 or 28, and claimed to have been all around the world, coming back to Basalt (not Aspen) "'cause it's the most beautiful place on the goddamn planet." A passionate hunter and fisherman, he'd frequently stop by and leave us fresh trout, venison steaks, or other tasty game. Although most folks knew Frank as a troublemaker, he was unfailingly polite and easygoing around us, and his gifts were greatly appreciated during the lean times. I read in the paper about a night Frank was out at the cowboy restaurant and dance-hall with someone else's wife when the husband took a rifle and shot Frank through the window, crippling him. Frank had come back from 'Nam whole only to end up paralyzed from the waist down by a bullet from another kind of enemy fire. He didn't live much longer after that, washing down a hundred or so painkillers with a bottle of whiskey. I couldn't say I blamed him. "Live fast and die young, leave a good looking corpse" wasn't just a hippie cliché, a naïve counterculture romance with self-destruction. For many of us it was a reality and an imperative. Hope I die before I get old, as Pete Townsend wrote. Maybe he was overstating the case, but countless minor legends were born as a result of adrenaline lives and premature toe-tags. The catch was that you weren't around to cash in on the benefits of your hard-won mythic stature.

That summer of 1969, the pipe for the city of Basalt water supply on Basalt Mountain needed much work, an emergency. Someone organized six or seven of us young guys who needed work to help the mayor, a W.C. Fields kind of character, to save the city water. This involved trenching and laying miles of new pipeline on the side of the mountain, mostly like a giant scree field. There was myself, Nick Ledder, Joe Poleski, Ben Meyers, and a couple of others. It was dirty, gritty hard work for not much pay but we were saving the little town's water. From then on we were accepted by the cowboys and the old boys and could drink in the Midland any time without worrying about trouble. It was like the end of the Cold War. The cowboys had made the monumental discovery that with a little smoke of the weed their new hippie drinking buddies provided their whiskey went a lot further. And when some of the looser hippie chicks decided to see if cowboys really stayed on longer, the cowboys became the most docile group of bad-actor rednecks you ever wanted to see. They doffed their Stetsons and brought candy and flowers to chicks who'd bake them hash brownies and wander around the house ass-naked except for a strand or two of turquoise beads dangling between gently bouncing tits. Detente was flourishing.

The crew we had on the pipeline was a good group. Nick Ledder had been the bar manager at Barnaby's in Chicago when my band played there and he was a good friend to us at that time. He had left Chicago months before I had, going to California to race motorcycles, which was his passion. After a couple of bad crashes and the destruction of his machine he somehow ended up in Aspen. He was living six miles up the valley from me across from the King Ranch, close to the pipeline.

We would finish work on the mountain and head to the Midland and try to finish off all the beer. Ben Meyers lived in a small cabin up the Frying Pan with his girlfriend, Mindy, a busty, freckle-faced brunette with a good attitude and pleasant manner. Ben was from back east somewhere and was probably 6'2" 250 or so, a gentle giant who always had a smile and laissez-faire demeanor. They were fun people to be around -- happy drunks and stoners, generous with their food, booze, and weed, as comfortable around the cowboys as they were with the freaks. Joe Poleski was stocky, balding, a Marine Corps veteran from Chicago who also was a good guy, capable and no-bullshit. He seemed to carry less psychic baggage than a lot of the other vets I knew, or maybe he just hid it better. He lived up the Frying Pan too, and we endured many adventures up and down the road courtesy of various subpar vehicles. Joe had a large, pure white German shepherd, Lobo, who went everywhere with his "dad."

At the base of Little Nell, the lowest part of the ski area on Aspen Mountain that ends right in town, was a building that housed a bar\restaurant originally called the Centre. This business was owned by John Dutton, a transplanted Chicagoan from a wealthy family.

John was a pleasant fellow, and the place did a brisk business, having rock and roll in the afternoons and evenings in the upstairs (ski hill level) with ski shops for retail and rentals downstairs. After I moved out from Chicago I realized that John was from the "street" there as well as one of his main bartenders, Nick Ledder, from Chicago and the pipeline crew. These guys knew and were friends with Big Phil (Phil Rapp, owner of Barnaby's as well as Mothers) and one of our band's managers. So I called Phil one day from Limp's ranch to let him know what was going on here and that there was action, and that some of his pals were here. One thing led to another and soon Phil arrived in Aspen, all 6'2" 350 lbs of him, and began to shake things up. He was a very energetic guy, a super hustler and a very funny person to be around. Eventually, he brought his money partners with him, and they bought in with Dutton.

The first order of business was to do a complete remodel in the rustic theme and build a subterranean nightclub, which became known as the Gallery. The Gallery (nicknamed The Night

Gallery) became the undisputed rock and roll late night action center of the whole local scene, and was actually the place where the Eagles put their group together, playing most of one summer there. The construction of the Gallery was done by Rapp, Ledder, Poleski, Hedford and myself, with occasional help from various others who were temporarily out of other work. The floor was done with railroad ties, the walls poured concrete faced with brick, and the bars and interiors all old barnwood and stained glass as was the style at the time. There were two bars, one at each end with a bandstand in the middle. The place was always packed and had more scenes, scams, rendezvous, hookups and such than one could imagine. The frenzy that occurred at two o'clock closing was what I coined as the "two o'clock shuffle." This was when the coyness, cuteness and games came to a compulsory finish. All cards were on the table and it was time to figure out who was going home with whom. I'm sure this is a ritual that was and is repeated all over the world in these types of places, but there was always a sense of urgency, almost desperation that was somehow moving. The "two o'clock shuffle" was probably the beginning of many marriages, and surely the end of an equal number. By helping with the summer work crew, I not only had some cash pay to live on, but the promise of a bartending job when the club opened in the fall. I even managed to book my bands into the club but unfortunately got stiffed out of my commission and wasn't strong enough to prevent the rip-off.

We had a good work crew at the new Little Nells with two upstairs bars and the Gallery open at night, with Ledder, myself, Eddie Plane, Root, and a couple other characters running the bars. Eddie was from Boston (*Bahstan*), a smallish guy with a quick wit and great sense of humor, not unlike most of the local residents. Root was a rangy Oklahoma cowboy with more country cornpone-isms than you could stand: "Christ on a cracker!" was one favorite oath; a less-than-well-endowed chick might be "flat as roadkill"; a novice, hopelessly inept skier was "trying to make chicken salad outa chicken shit." Root could crack you up to the point of pain with his homespun phrases.

One of the big summer events was the local rodeo, a chance for all the wannabe cowboys to compete (or so they thought) with the real cowboys on the circuit that were there. This was somewhat of a local tradition, a gut check, a chance for some to prove the magnitude of their gonads. The day was usually a drunken blur of a dusty party, with a new accumulation of bumps and bruises. One time, however, things turned decidedly more lethal and tragic. First, Eddie Plane had decided that he was going to be a bull rider. I don't know if he had been drinking or what, but on his first ride he drew a particularly randy bull. In a matter of seconds, the beast had dislodged Eddie and slammed him into the wooden fence. Poor Eddie was knocked unconscious, and went into a coma, which lasted for days, leaving him much diminished. Bad as that was, it wasn't the worst the day had to offer. After the event, a car-full of drunk locals ran off a cliff on the Woody Creek road, killing three and seriously injuring a couple of others. A very dark day, but as usual, the party continued.

Though a lower-key existence than we'd

enjoyed in Aspen, our life down valley was far from dull. We discovered several favorite destinations from various side trips around the area, when weather permitted. One of the standouts was the Redstone Hot Springs, which was on the Crystal River a few miles out of Carbondale, another sleepy old burg between Redstone and Glenwood Springs up by Mt. Sopris. While Glenwood boasts the world's largest outdoor hot pool, which is also a wonderful thing, the Redstone Hot Springs was of a different place and time. Mystical. The Crystal River runs from Mt. Sorpris and fresh springs, and is an ice-cold, fast-moving, and powerful body of water that cuts a fairly narrow canyon. Along this at an elevation near 8000 feet there is a hot mineral spring that flows out of the rocks into a river in a bright blue bubbling stream. Right along the bank had been dug a pool about eight feet long, six feet wide and about four and a half feet deep that the mineral water flowed into. The pool was constructed of logs and mortar and was built right into the cement floor of the cement bathhouse that covered it. You had to park by the road and walk down a gravel path about fifty yards and probably one hundred feet lower. There was a steel door on the building and pool etiquette at the time was widely known. If there were no cars already parked and no sounds coming from the bathhouse your whole group could go in, disrobe, hang your clothes on the rack of sixteen penny nails, and hop in. The hop part of that was only a hop in tortoise time. The water was so hot that it took several minutes to ease all the way in. The challenge was to stay in as long as you could stand to, maybe fifteen minutes the first time, then clamber out and run about ten feet to the river and take a plunge. Then when your teeth were rattling out of your skull, you went back in and this time leaped into the hot water. Talk about a sizzle. After three or four rounds you could end up just looking out the door across the water at the little pasture and steep wall of the canyon for quite a while. The buzz would last for hours and made the twenty-some miles drive home daunting at times. Driving under the Influence of Insanity.

If, upon your arrival, there were already

cars parked, hence people inside, the procedure was to call out, "Hello, how are ya? Four of us here." The answer could be either that they would be out soon, or something like, "There's plenty of room — come on in!" The unique part of the custom was that groups took the plunge together with no regard to age, race, gender, or clothing. This had been the custom for as long as anybody could remember, the story being that the pool was originally a ceremonial bath of the Ute Indians, and had been frequented by the local ranch folk for many years. Some nights were busy with lots of hippies, local and otherwise; you could meet some cool people while naked in the thick hot water. Or if you'd just come to the pool with your old lady, the candles brought in at night made for an unforgettable intimate experience. Leave the flowers and candy to the cowpokes; making it in that steaming water with candleflame flickering against both your bodies was sensual nirvana. Even without the added rush of sex, to hold your breath and totally submerge, sitting on the bottom, was a religious epiphany. The sounds of the gurgling springs brought ancient images to mind, striking so deep as to be genuinely moving. The gulf of centuries effaced, you felt a dizzying continuity with the long-past, its people and rituals. Ego wafted away and you ceased, at least for a little while, to be *you*; instead, you were as still and right as a tile in a timeless mosaic. This was truly one of those spiritual places with a natural power that was staggering. Day or night, a trip to the hot springs was always a good idea, and always an "A" ticket ride.

After the first winter in Aspen, with high season and the tourist dollars supporting all us restaurant workers nicely, the move not only down-valley, but into the serious off season was a real shocker. Out of season was not only the skiing, but the tourist dollars that made the lifestyle in winter so easy. Here I was in the old west, with not many ways to make a living, I mean it was scratching time to even eat well. This was a switch from my Chicago rock and roll "star" existence where I had everything I needed, and then some, all the time. All of a sudden, I needed to pay attention to every penny, and get tired, dirty and sweaty to even have a few of those. From elite to construction laborer to wannabe carpenter (for the $10/hr)was not a pleasant transition, and there I was. It was real hard to survive then, and it became clear why one didn't become a local until living through all the seasons. Many more passed through and kept moving than those that stuck it out, so now it made sense why nobody wanted to invest time and energy in a friendship or other relationship that would disappear momentarily.

At the Wooden Handle, there were five year-round cabins across the road from the river on the hillside next to the owner's house that were rented out year round. The old square-cut log homesteaders cabin right next to the big house was what we had lucked into, a nice one bedroom with insulation, a big kitchen, really a cozy place. The other four were one room small cabins, not nearly as comfortable. And across the road were four summer cabins right on the river, which although frozen and closed in the winter, were delightful in summer with decks overhanging the Frying Pan River, which was about thirty feet across at that point, a fast moving trout-laden stream that put up a constant roar that made the cabins very special. These were rented to a group of hippies that did leather work and of course became friends, especially with Sparrow who was becoming better and better at her beading and leather creations which she had begun to make. And of course there were two or three of these hippies chicks that were great looking and were always hitting on me. I did get to one of them, but missed a couple that I really thought I should have. So little time, so much to do.

One of our joys was a Malamute-Husky-wolf mix we named Pablo we got when he was six weeks old. His litter was hiding under a garage like fugitives, which was what the owner of the mama dog was, a local named Dan Tollman gone on the lam after getting busted with a big load of weed. The local sheriff, Art Smith, wanted to kill the pups as they were very skittish, almost feral, but public sentiment prevailed to commute their sentence. Pablo was black and white with a tight curled tail, and he grew up to about 100 pounds. He gradually got over his shyness and became a great dog, very friendly and playful. One of his siblings was taken by Ray, a California hippie pot dealer who lived six miles up the road at the King Ranch. This big, shaggy guy, Nanuck, used to run down the road to our place, pick up Pablo, and the two of them would run off and disappear for days at a time. When they finally showed up they were always filthy and bedraggled, but I guess they had a good time. One of the small cabins above was rented by Michael, my old guitar player, and his girlfriend Laurie, who had followed us out from Chicago.

Though Michael had helped us with the Centre construction, and had done some work on a couple pick up jobs with me, he wasn't really suited for this line of work, either physically or mentally. I managed to get him a small gig playing at the Hotel Jerome in the afternoons, and though he was building a following as he was an extremely talented singer and musician, soon he headed out to LA to start another band and record. We had worked together for a couple years, and it was kind of a drag to see him go, but we were all bouncing around so much then that lots of people appeared and were gone, some to be hooked up with again, others not to be seen again. The pace.

Soon it was fall 1969, the awful summer was over and the town started to buzz with the anticipation of another ski and tourist season. I couldn't believe that I had been in Colorado for a whole year. While some of the time had really seemed to drag, a whole year had gone by, and it seemed now that it was more like a blink. I had the better bartender job at the Centre (now named Little Nells), and Sparrow had gotten on at North Beach Leathers, as a salesperson and also selling her custom beaded items that she was now quite skilled at. I got a part time job at the Highlands bar which included a free ski pass there, so I started stumbling around the mountain a little, though I had no idea what I was supposed to do, I just knew that the speed rush somehow made up for the bruises my many crashes produced. We just worked and got through that winter, until spring of 1970 hit, and once again, at Easter everything came to a grinding halt, and we were no more prepared for it than the year before. It was nice to finally be mostly accepted as a local and I had skied enough to want more, but now the tourists and their dollars were gone again, it was a ghost town, and what were we going to live on now. This was really getting old. One of the Basalt guys I had met was a hippie dude name Gene, who along with his parents, kids, brothers and extended family owned the local dry cleaning plant which serviced the whole valley, and was located right in Basalt, next to the cowboy bar. Well Gene was a pot smoker like most of us and claimed to have moved lots of loads from his Tucson connections up to Salt Lake City where he was from. Since there was a local drought that May of 1970, and I was broke, and since my new local kid Aspen friends had money and liked to move weed, a plan was hatched. My buddy Mike Larkin arranged to have some of the Green Acres (section of Aspen locals) boys put up $4000 and we were off to Tucson to meet Gene's lady connection. All mixed metaphors aside, talk about a keystone cops, Chinese fire drill wild goose chase. After spending a couple days of expenses trying to locate this gal, when we finally found her she said that most of the load had gotten busted and there weren't enough bricks to go around. Shit. We were just hanging out at a local bar playing pool bitching about this when we met up with a local regular named Tony who said he could help us out. A cross between a B movie gangster and some kind of juvenile delinquent, Tony shuttled us around the suburbs and barrios of Tucson in his tricked out Charger yelling, waving a pistol and shooting through the open windows, just a real class act. But for all his swagger and noise he came up with no weed, only a lump of white substance the nature of which we could never really determine. So we bought a 1964 Pontiac Grand Prix from a little used car lot and headed north on our long ride back to Colorado. To cap off this week long exercise in futility, when I finally got back to the cabin about three a.m. I found one of my old pals from Michigan and Chicago, Burt, in my bed with Sparrow. As I noisily stumbled in the door they were all scurrying and insisted they weren't doing anything, but of course that didn't explain why old Burt hadn't been on the couch. So now my possessive, loyal old lady had a somewhat different look to me, and I knew my days of feeling guilty over my wandering eye were done. And of course the white stuff was worthless, nobody liked the Grand Prix, which we had to run down to Denver and trade for a Ford pickup and some cash, and still no one was happy and we were assholes. Quite an auspicious beginning to my trafficking career.

That summer, in July 1970, the hippies by the river had secured some backing from a wealthy Boston father, and left to go to Wellesley to open a leather shop, Geppettos, which became a success in the upscale college town. Somehow they took Sparrow with them, to help with the store. This left me alone for a while, which left me free to do the hippies that were left behind, which was very good. But also, love beckoned, and we made plans for myself and Pablo, who was over a year old and a beautiful black and white curled tail Malamute to fly to Boston to join up with the clan.

So I built a kennel of plywood and heavy duty screen (master carpenter that I was in my own mind) gave Pablo some doggie downers that I got from the vet, loaded him up and hopped a plane. The flight, though long, seemed uneventful until we landed at Logan in Boston, and were taxiing, when the captain made the announcement "Will the passenger who has a dog on the plane please report to the stewardess at the front of the cabin". Of course I feared for my dog, but it would turn out that fear of the dog was the real drill. After being led off the plane and taken to the tarmac under the plane, the situation finally was explained to me. It seems that sometime during the flight, Pablo had recovered from the double dose of downers, had chewed and broken out of his kennel, and was roaming loose in the baggage compartment. Being a Malamute, he was also howling nonstop, which alarmed the pilot, who thought maybe he had a hydraulic leak or some such malfunction. Fairly stressful, I'm sure. Then after landing, when the baggage handlers opened the hatch above them to remove the baggage, here was this 100 lb black and white at the opening looking down at them with lots of teeth and big dilated eyes. They were afraid to do anything except call the idiot in charge of the animal. That was me. Of course, once Pablo saw me there, he hopped down all happy, and we went our merry way. Welcome to Boston.

We had a big nice house there, very clean, with everyone working hard, me moving furniture for a used furniture barn that bought up estates all over town and brought a truckload a day back to the Dover Country Store, where a crowd waited to buy it up. A very interesting operation owned and operated by a Mrs. Wakefield, a blue-blood flinty New Englander, who worked tirelessly, was sharp as a tack, and extremely fair-minded and goodhearted. And we all went to the Maharishi retreat and were initiated into transcendental meditation. Vegetarian, no drugs, clean wholesome living at its finest. I was good for about two or three months before I had to get back to the mountains, taking Sparrow and Pablo in a free delivery car and drove cross country, mostly non-stop, finally getting back to the valley.

I suppose that the greatest irony at that time was that while Sparrow and I had moved to Basalt to escape the messy domestic situation at Limpy's, our own relationship was well on its way to extinction. We shared equal blame, I guess, for our deterioration. Sparrow was young, after all, and her chief means of demonstrating her mad love for me was through extreme affection, jealousy and possessiveness. Not that I didn't give her plenty of cause; I was tempted constantly by the smorgasbord of hot babes in Aspen, and in those days self-control wasn't exactly my strong suit. Although we maintained a degree of civility, the anxiety level was high. As we both worked in town, we would drive in together, each go to our own jobs, and hook up to drive back down-valley and home. There were several times when I ended up in the arms of some fuck-bunny when I was supposed to be meeting Sparrow to head home. She would be frantically searching town for me, and more than one close call had me on edge. Once, while rifling for dropped change in the backseat of the Mustang, Sparrow discovered an unfamiliar pair of panties, evidence of a furtive, drunken encounter the week before between me and a giddy Aspen cocktail waitress whose name I didn't even remember. Like any adulterer worth his salt I tried to lie my way out of it: I'd found the panties in the parking lot of the laundromat, I insisted, and tossed them into the car believing they were "ours." She didn't buy it. Sparrow was a sweet person, sexy and giving and fun to be with, but monogamy was not my style at this time. Was I a callous asshole? Sure. I hadn't come to Aspen to hone my moral consciousness, and the town was only too happy to oblige. Increasingly distraught and paranoid, Sparrow took to threatening suicide on an almost nightly basis. Her gestures ranged from the melodramatic to the downright annoying, but luckily didn't seem in earnest. She chopped off her waist-length hair to *Rosemary's Baby* dimensions; she hurled most of my clothes outside onto the snowy ground; and most memorably, though at the time no laughing matter, while I dozed, half-drunk, in a chair, she doused my Frye boots with lighter fluid and tried to set them on fire. Thank God the gas smell sobered me up in time. Eventually, I managed to arrange for her to take a trip to San Francisco to stay with friends from Chicago, Barry and Annette. They had a leather shop in North Beach, and hired Sparrow to do custom beading and make moccasins. While there she took up with Barry's younger brother Pat. They were well-suited to each other and ended up marrying. Guess it didn't take too long for Sparrow to figure out she was well rid of me, and to be honest, vice-versa. I hope Pat either stayed faithful to her or else took out an insurance policy on his footwear. In 1970, housing was so limited that the only way to find a house or apartment to rent was to know someone who was moving and get turned on to that place. This often involved pecking order, one-upmanship and sometimes being able to "out-local" any other aspirants. Residence in the valley for at least a full season was required for local status, but having lived there for more years than another local gave one even better credentials. Now that I had achieved the single status I needed I was ready to move back up to Aspen the better to explore my newfound freedom. I was lucky enough to be friends with Buzz Williams, who was moving to Denver, and he offered Pablo and me his studio apartment in town.

With Sparrow and the Mustang that had brought us west gone, so were the last tangible traces of my old life in Chicago. It would be easy now to claim regret or nostalgia. Easy, but bullshit. The truth is that I felt liberated, reborn, even. Baptized by dope and snow into the Aspen Church of Unfettered Do-Your-Own-Thing, I admit I was an easy convert. And like most converts, single-minded and a bit overzealous. Praise Be To Christ Jesus, and let the games begin.

Did we really say
how much we would pay
for what games we play
or in our own heads stay
for another day
with no concern for the way
things on others we lay
for just another day

CHAPTER 4:

At Last in 'Improper' Aspen Proper

Being in town after two years of wanting to was like being a kid in a candy store. My little studio apartment on the second floor of a triplex just off rt 82 on the east end of town was perfect for Pablo and me. I had parking for two cars, a good next- door neighbor, Steve Squires, a waiter at the Mother lode, and a somewhat daffy German landlady, Margaret, who cared about nothing except collecting her rents. I felt so free after all that time with an "old lady," and was thrilled to be right in town, in the thick of it, unfettered, just cruising with my dog partner, looking for all the excitement and good times I could manage, right along with most of the town. The apartment came partially furnished, and I brought a couple of things I had, a stereo with my records, an old Volvo 544 I was driving, and a ten speed Peugeot bicycle that I had picked up for $50 from a waitress who couldn't use it with her broken leg. So I was pretty well set up and being right in town, had found work with a contractor trying to finish up a couple houses before the snow started to fly. This was the closest to some kind of job security I had found here, and I started to fall into a routine, which was to last through the holidays, finishing up the interiors after the roof and windows were in and the snow was falling.

So fall of 1970 turned into winter of 1971, and by the end of January, I was back at the Highlands bar for après-ski work with pretty good tips, and of course my free ski pass. I was starting to get the idea that you were supposed to make the skis turn, not just go straight down, thereby gaining some measure of control and chance for survival. What a concept. With more skiing, there were also more people to meet, especially chicks, who seemed to pay no attention to any guys except the expert skiers. I knew then that I had to become a good skier for several reasons, not the least being a level of social acceptance that I had been used to as a rock n roller and needed now. For most of that winter, though, I just kind of faked it, trying not to get hurt, because I lacked the funds to take lessons, and the whole thing was still very new to me, so I was a little frustrated, a lot scared, but still was completely drawn in by the thrill and good feeling of the sport.

One of the "legitimate" activities in town was called "pub-sitting," hanging around in the Pub, The Jerome B. Wheeler Public House drinking beer, the classic subterranean "pub" under the historic Wheeler Opera House. There almost seemed to be a certain number of hours per week required to insure one's "local" credentials, and thus group acceptance. One day Nutty Ned and Gloves got started on a strange session of "pub-sitting," for and by what means still remain unknown. They were at the table nearest the kitchen, just the two of them and a constant supply of pitchers. Now Ned was real big and tough, but his good buddy Gloves was a smallish guy, a crackerjack mechanic who worked at old Martin Bishop's garage. Gloves was from New York and drove an old 65 Oldsmobile. The keys were permanently in the ignition and anyone he knew had standing permission to use the car whenever it was needed. "Hey Gloves, can I use your car?" was asked on almost a daily basis. And Gloves would always reply in the same casual manner, "If it's still parked out front, no problem. If not, someone else must have it." At times when Gloves wanted to go home but didn't have his car available, he would just shrug and walk the few blocks to his home, Tragedy Manor, which was in the small industrial section by the river and shared the same small junkyard of Bishop's garage for a front yard, where Gloves "real" ride lived, a beat up '48 Lincoln Continental Convertible.

Anyway, this particular day's bar sport was even more borderline-nonsensical than usual. They would sit and drink for a time in silence, then Ned would mutter "you bastard" and haul off and kick Gloves, sometimes knocking him off his chair. They'd sit and drink some more, then Gloves would pick up this little billy-club he had with him, lean across the table and give Ned a whack across the shoulder. Silently, they would go back to drinking. After this had gone on for several hours, Kendall was getting a little worried and somehow talked them into taking it someplace else. There was never any explanation regarding what happened, and I'm sure most of us really didn't want to know what had inspired the peculiar little game. In Aspen insanity, like good looks, was a given.

I have another vivid memory involving Gloves and Ned, a little more serious but still with an element of the bizarre whimsy that characterized them. Gloves and I had gone to Pueblo, driving through a bitch of a snowstorm, on a mission of mercy to a hospital for the mentally challenged, where Ned's attorney had arranged his punishment time for the big brawl wherein he'd broken the chick's nose and beaten the shit out of her male protectors. A loony bin was preferable to a prison, Ned's lawyer had figured. Although his was to be a short stay, Ned had called Gloves to bring him some cigarettes and socks, and Gloves talked me into making the run, probably because I had never seen much of that part of the state.

In Aspen at that time there had been a minor bar mystery going on for a while. Round silver and black stickers near the size of a golfball had been appearing stuck with some kind of space shuttle glue to stools, chairs, bars, walls, phones, cars and generally all over Aspen. The only word on them was OP-TOPS. They were obviously promotional gimmicks from one of the ski business vendors, but who had gotten them, from where, and was stickering the town was unknown, even un-rumored. So here Gloves and I were bringing Ned his socks and smokes, and as we were registering at the hospital's reception desk the first thing we saw was one of those goofy OP-TOP stickers on the end of the counter. We looked at each other and started cracking up so bad the nurse likely thought we were potentially more than just visitors.

As for Ned, he seemed to have regressed to about an eleven-year-old level, having a good old time categorizing and lightly messing with the heads of his new housemates. "See that dude?" he said, pointing out a raggedy, Orphan-Annie-eyed hippie shuffling by, "He's got the shizo-affect shit, they say. But if you ask me, he either got dosed on some high-octane acid or else sure as hell ought to be!" When another inmate, a gap-toothed kid of maybe 24, stammered vaguely to us, "I hope . . . I hope . . . I hope I exist," Ned rejoined, "I hope you do too, man, 'cause if not, get the fuck out of my hallucination!" In short, Ned didn't appear the least traumatized by incarceration. He was plainly glad to see us and pleased with himself for not having to receive his visitors in a more overtly penal environment. His biggest concern was that we would talk back in town and let his OP-TOP cat right out of the bag. After making brother promises that we wouldn't rain on his parade, we left the state hospital and headed for the blizzard on Loveland, where as we chained up, the Highway Patrol made it barely past us. We got the chains on and cleared the summit. That night it felt good to be back tucked into the Pub drinking cold beer. It was cool to know that the hospital hadn't broken Ned; hell, he'd seemed no more than mildly inconvenienced. But lockup was lockup, and I found myself savoring my freedom along with my beer.

Then all at once it seemed like it was spring, the snow was melting, town was a mudbowl, all the tourists were gone, most of the restaurants and bars were closed, the ghost town look again. But this year, it didn't seem quite so bad somehow. There were a few more places staying open, and there was a lot more early building going on. As April turned into May you could hear the chain saws, skills saws and hammers going all day and the town was building again. And now I had a foreman job building an addition on the Continental Inn, prefabbing all the walls and making our own concrete beams for the underground garage the rooms would sit on. This was a very different kind of project being run by the hotel owner, Hans Cantrup, who owned several lodges and was a very clever German immigrant who knew how to cut every corner, bend every rule and generally exploit the building code system to an unheard of degree. He seemed to always be getting fined for some code violation or other, but by the time he had to pay, he had collected so much in room rentals that the fines were a mere pittance. So town was cooking in the spring of 1971 and I had work, had grown my hair down to my shoulders, had my dog and was becoming a true local. Wow. Much as I had liked Sparrow, I gave her little thought and it felt real good to be on my own, cruising.

Cruising was done in trucks, jeeps, cars, on cycles and ten-speeds. A ten-speed was really the best means by which to get around. Lots of the streets were not paved and there were alleys and paths that were only sometimes passable, not always totally clear of snow, logs, fallen trees, building materials or whatnot. You could go to work, to the store, movies, or hit on a girl all on your bike. Of course, there were many local athletes who had serious bicycles and used them for intensive training. Going for a ride with one of these guys could be a major ego-bust. Usually a ride involved at least a small group and there was an unspoken rule that a seemingly casual jaunt would be a test of some kind, though rarely a formally defined race. Nevertheless, you sensed that it would not be cool to get left too far in the dust. Right. Pedaling a comfy Peugeot town bike up a grade around 9-10,000 feet above sea level chasing a rabbit on a flyweight titanium frame road race bike was a prescription for humility. When your lungs and legs are on fire, you can hardly breathe, and you're starting to become dizzy, it's time to accept that you are not going to be able to keep the pace. For a good workout all you had to do was start at Main Street, put your bike in the highest gear and head up Durant or one of the north-south streets running from Main right up to Aspen Mountain where they could dead end into a ski run or a parking lot. Making it to the top in high gear was a pump, regardless of the type of bike you were on. Then you would turn around, point downhill, stand up on the pedals, lock your knees into the seat, put your arms at your side, lean forward like a ski jumper and let 'er rip. Top speed was probably only about 50 or 60, but when combined with the challenge of passing through three or four fairly busy intersections the thrill factor could be worthy of the Wide World of Sports.

One other short-lived sport was bicycle broomball. Although this one, played in a parking lot, was also exhilarating, the damage inflicted on both the bikes and riders exceeded the enjoyment. Guys who had been successfully negotiating expert ski trails for years were busting arms and collarbones playing parking lot polo. Mostly, the bike was used for everyday transportation, especially if some stealth was required, such as when you were scouting out a new chick or making a discreet drug score. One day when I was cruising town on my bike, I stopped at Ted Roof's bike shop to fix the polo damage. Stopped there also was a shapely female cyclist in a tank top and skimpy shorts I'd never met before. We clicked. After a short cruise Linda Lou and I ended up at the rented condo where Hedford was staying and fell totally in love on the floor of the guest bedroom. The bicycle as pick-up rig. And the exercise sure made for some limber riding elsewhere, too. We then moved into CC Edgefield's extra bedroom in her house on the fifth hole of the golf course. CC was just divorced from Peter Edgefield, a developer, contractor, PR man, etc., so she was pretty comfortable along with her five-year-old daughter, Sissy. CC's was a new crowd for me, mostly University of Colorado Boulder people, a sophisticated hard-partying gang who seemed individually and collectively to have nothing in life more important than having a wild time. My kind of folks. The parties there were outrageous screamers where you could end up with permanent facial damage from laughing too much. And who ended up in the hot tub with whom was a source of constant amazement. Life on the golf course was a new chapter in decadence for me, as Linda Lou and CC, both Boulder grads, were free-spirited and partied with a vengeance. Hangovers and their various chemical cure-alls were the order of the day at the house, but CC was also a dedicated mother and Sissy's needs always came first. We might have all been carousing until dawn, but CC always had a hot breakfast for Sissy and a pleasant ride to kindergarten. CC, or Moms as she was called, was the ringleader of the UC-Boulder group. Since these kids had pretty much grown up in or near the mountains, they were all skiers. Bob Beattie, Beats to his friends, had coached the Colorado ski team and had started World Pro Skiing, the circuit that has two skiers skiing parallel courses simultaneously. This format brings lots of excitement to the hill, sort of like drag-racing on skis. Spider Sabich was probably the most successful of the Beats' coached crew. From the Lake Tahoe area, Spider was a natural athlete who trained ski racing with his brother Steve

(Pinky) since childhood. Spider had been on the Olympic ski team and when the pro circuit began he was the first champion of that series. Blond and good looking, Spider had an easygoing manner and was extremely popular, being a good guy who liked to have lots of fun. He was a natural target for all manner of ski groupies and took his duty seriously, maybe to his own eventual undoing. Pinky, who was also a good skier, a notch below Spider on the competitive scale, was also a good guy, very much up to the Boulder party pace and still a little laid-back, a real low-key person. Both Spider and Steve were accomplished pilots and shared a Piper twin Aztec that was kept at the airport ready for quick trips to wherever their whims dictated.

One night in June of '71 was particularly remarkable. CC's long-lost buddy, Randy, had shown up from Central America. It seemed as if Randy had driven through jungles and mountains straight through to Aspen. He had a WWII military Dodge Power Wagon that was set up heavy duty in camo, more like a tank than a truck, really. The whole gang went cruising downtown after consuming mind-numbing amounts of tequila, beer and Panama Red. We were roaring: Linda Lou, CC, Pinky, Lackey, Buzzy Ware and some other chicks. Randy had a monster stereo in the car with four-foot-high concert speakers and I don't know how many hundred watts too much of power. With hot salsa music blasting like a rock concert and a truck full of crazies, we set off for downtown at a lurching seven miles per hour. Naturally, all activity at our select stops came to a halt, the noise was that earsplitting.

As we made our way around the circuit of bars we were really having a good time, and it seemed to us that we were spreading joy everywhere we went. A loud, obnoxious, cuss-filled kind of joy, but joy nonetheless. After a couple of laps we attracted the attention of the Aspen Police Department. When the nice officer on foot asked us to stop, Randy did so and appeared to want to be obliging. But in response to the usual questions about licenses, registration and the like, Randy just yelled "What the FUCK?" This went on for a couple of minutes, Randy looking concerned for the baffled policeman and the rest of us breaking up.

Finally Randy bellowed at the cop that he couldn't hear him because the music was too loud. This was too much for all of us and CC started begging Randy to let up. "For Christ's sake, you're gonna get us all busted!" I for one was sure we were all going to jail. Finally CC prevailed upon him to cut the music. Now it sounded like EF Hutton was about to speak. Miraculously Randy produced the proper documents and since there was no law against going too slow, we were allowed to proceed with the promise that there would be no more trouble or we would go to jail. That the cop seemed oblivious to our obvious booziness said a lot about the generally laissez-faire attitude of Aspen law enforcement in those days.

My encounter with Linda Lou on my bicycle was my first clue that the bike could be an effective tool for getting laid. Some of the other tools were pretty evident then. If one had a good deal of wealth, then, as always, there seemed to be no shortage of hot chicks available. Another passport to sexual success was having a good job -- either a ski instructor position or a good bartending job qualified. Just being a cool skier could assure a degree of success regardless of position or economic accomplishment. Still another effective aphrodisiac was having a part in the purveyance or transportation of illegal substances, especially since this "work" included a ready stash of product. These seemed to be the criteria the women held important, good looks being a given, since for some reason almost all the locals were to some degree athletic and most were attractive. The "beautiful people" of Aspen. Of course, it helped that the women were as openly horny as the men and sometimes became much more aggressive. Conquests were not so much achievements, notches on the gun belt, as mutual acknowledgment that everybody pretty much wanted the same thing: to get laid. The protocol could be deceptively simple. When you and a lady met, and there was attraction, smiles and such, "Hey, you wanna go smoke a doob?" was the key question, the place where the scene would start or not. This was the first shared intimacy, the ice-breaker, the first step on the steamy journey. Pot was as the coin of the realm, subtle, light, mostly non-threatening and at that time readily available at little or sometimes no cost.

This was an innocent time, the shared joint still the opener, the ice-breaker is still a good vibe. The pot business was flourishing in the U.S. then, and it seemed like everyone who lived in town was involved in one way or another. Linda Lou told me about some residents who had big sailboats in Florida or elsewhere along the east coast. These folks would be out of town sometimes for months on end and return with new trucks, cars, and ready cash for prime real estate. And many of the locals had told me they fed their families shuffling truck loads of weed crosstown to out-of-state purchasers who seemed to flock into Aspen from all over to score. There were those who looked at this activity as their regular employment and prided themselves on their reputations for being righteous, reliable dealers, not rip-off artists, who always paid the bill for their fronted bales. Three-quarter-ton four-wheel-drive Ford pickups with a camper shell were called "stuffers" because you could load upwards of 1000 pounds of weed in them and haul off to whatever city you had a market in. For a while this activity was very quiet; you never heard about it or heard about trouble. That would change, though, and soon someone would tell me about airplanes being apprehended at small airports in the vicinity of town, then larger busts all over the three-state area, usually involving some Aspen residents. Some of these folks were of the serious opinion that they were righteous people because they refused to deal in cocaine, and would handle only pot. Their reasoning was that despite misguided laws to the contrary, marijuana was a non-lethal, beneficial natural substance. But regardless of their desire to not traffic in harmful substances, when the heat came down they were sentenced just as harshly, if not more so than their coke-dealing brethren. Some of the busts came as a real surprise to many, for those apprehended were not known as dealers, sometimes having so good a cover that their involvement was almost impossible to glean. One hit that was a real shocker was when Nick Ledder and Hunter Hyman got nailed in New Mexico unloading a DC6 on a deserted airstrip. Nick was always steadily employed as a bartender and didn't seem to fit the profile of a drug dealer. But in those days, few of us did.

What started to happen with me, like many of my friends, was that someone would say they needed some weed and had money for a half-pound, or six ounces or whatever. Then I would bump into another buddy playing pool or skiing or something and he would say "No problem, I've still got a half of some killer left." So I could take the bag to the guy who wanted to buy it, pay the other for the whole thing, and have a nice stash left for myself for free. This action just kind of started to be regular, and I thought I just was being clever in having my free weed, never considering myself a dealer. And not just me either, this was seemingly an approved acceptable style for most of the town, from the bus boys to the lawyers, club owners, real estate brokers, etc. There seemed to be some kind of rule that if you were just trying to arrange your own stash, as opposed to making money, you were an innocent, a non-dealer, just a savvy consumer. We never thought about the consequences of the law, which would have had not so benign a view of this activity, even in 1971.

Another surprise involved my partner,

Rick Hedford, who had made the migration from Chicago with Sparrow and me. Rick was a Fiji brother at Kent State, the fifth or sixth college he had attended. He was an intense person, very personable but with more than a hint of mischief to him. To call him in college a hellraiser was an understatement. Rumor had it that he had been expelled from all the other colleges for an assortment of pranks and schemes gone awry, one supposedly resulting in the burning down of a barn. Nothing too serious – George Dubya kind of stuff. At Kent, he suffered a severe crash on his motorcycle that peeled his scalp, leaving him thin on top thereafter. As he was a very handsome guy, this must have been difficult for him, and though always fun-loving and high-spirited, Rick's temper lay buried not too deep. He could be worked up and made to go off like a firecracker, which some of the gang viewed as good bar sport. Hedford was very industrious, though, and had managed to purchase a lease and health food business that included a small restaurant room. He worked this gig diligently and efficiently, and acquired the nickname

"Captain Birdseed." He and his girlfriend Betsy had rented a little chalet on Hopkins St. owned by Therese Donald, one of the established real estate brokers in town. This cozy little scene was suddenly interrupted one Saturday morning when Rick's newest pot customers turned out to be employees of DEA. It seems that Rick had hooked up with a local stockbroker from Southern California, Donnie McGunn, and had been making commercial flights to San Diego and returning with suitcases of bricks of Mexican weed. Big surprise in town: two ostensibly straight businessmen now the apprehended pot dealers. Hedford lost his nerve, copped a plea and moved back east not long after.

In one other instance that became part of local lore, a local policeman, Dave Zimmerman, became a little overzealous in his duties and took it upon himself to raid the house of one of the long-time locals and confiscate some marijuana plants. At the time, this activity was considered overkill by the locals and was highly unusual. Within several weeks the officer's personal motorcycle had mysteriously blown up, and Zimmerman had had a large amount of LSD surreptitiously added to his beer one day. For months after that he wandered around town babbling, then finally took off for nobody seemed to know where. Hence the local caveat, "Be careful you don't park on top of no volcanos."While Zimmerman had probably been given a massive dose, "dropping," as it was called, for a time was quite the fad and considered a sport undertaken in good fun. The game usually involved dropping one of your buddies while he was tending bar. Then the innocent-acting beer drinkers at the bar could watch the effects. As the victim started to come on to the acid and everything started to move around and change colors, the boys at the bar would be breaking into laughter. Eventually the poor guy would figure out that somebody had gotten him. Depending upon the strength of the dose the bartender would either work through it, trying to act like nothing was wrong and thereby spoiling his pals' fun, or call in a sub and get the hell out from behind the bar. While theoretically this was a dangerous game, no one to my knowledge was ever seriously hurt or tripped out, how or why I'll never know. And the cop, after all, had had it coming to him; that had been an act of self-defense, according to local rationale. Rather, "Bar Wars" in town were always outrageous and usually benign. Not even the victims seemed to bear any hard feelings.

Now being in town was starting to feel natural, after a couple of years on the scene, I was an accepted part of the landscape, and I began to feel like a real local. I seemed to spend most of my time with a group of kids over in the Green Acres area, my pal Wingbat, Mike Clark, Greg Smart, Jeffrie McAllister, Gordon Smith, George Bailey, Tina Rubey, Mary Smart, Harriet Garth, just a whole bunch of people that grew up in Aspen. I think on some level I figured if I wanted to become a real local, I needed to learn the lay of the land from the natives, so to speak. And what a fun education it was from as interesting cast of unlikely characters as could be asked for. All the guys were motorheads, cars, jeeps, dirt bikes, and trucks included, and all seemed to be pretty fair backyard mechanics, and there was lots of swapping, dealing, buying and selling action going on. We were kind of a rag tag bunch of would be used car dealers. There was a bit of cash to be picked up by buying and fixing, or just buying right and selling to another local who needed wheels. It was really quite humorous and there were actually some spectacular (?) scores made. We would take a trip to Denver and pick up the Denver Post and the Rocky Mountain News, go for breakfast and scan the used car ads. Then a roll of quarters for the phone, many qualifying calls, a put together plan of attack, then off to the suburbs to grind on the sellers that we had isolated. Usually by the end of the day we would have our one or two Caddies or pickups, and be headed to our road race back to town. About a four hour drive back from Denver over passes through the mountains run as an enduro type of road race could get dicey and we had some real battles. Fortunately good fortune prevailed over good sense. At some point, I figured out how to work the dealers and concentrated on the closer metropolis of Glenwood Springs (a mere 40 mile drive) and did real well for a while with the Jeep dealer there. On one such occasion, I picked up a 52 Ford pickup that I watched the old cowboy original owner trade in, and a 61 International short wide half ton for $350 for the pair. The

Ford was a jewel, a little flathead V8 that ran like a top, and which Ted Roof talked me out of for $350. The International only had about 60 thousand miles and was like a new truck. This one I kept and drove for years, but more importantly, now Pablo had his truck to ride in.

With a truck for my dog, a cowboy hat, and some Frye boots, I really was a local, I thought, and at least didn't feel all the time like a stranger in a strange land. And the party pace was picking up quite a bit too. There were so many cute chickies and so little time, I was busy a lot, mostly with the local girls, but every once in a while you could pick up on a tourist from anywhere, everybody wanted a little fun. And Pablo went with me everywhere, work, to drink, party, he would be off running on his own sometimes for a couple of days, then just turn up outside the window of where I was, even if I was someplace and with someone that neither of us had ever been or met before. He would just be there looking in the window at you. Real special, but there were lots of special dogs in town.

A unique part of Aspen culture then was the dogs. All locals had at least one. Your dog went every place with you, work, play, to the bars, the movies, the bank. You could tell the few places that wouldn't allow dogs inside by the pack in front, lots of them hanging out of the cars or trucks. The best of them had lived in town for a while and were as familiar characters as their owners, in some cases even more so. Many dogs were known by people who did not know their masters. "Look, there's Buddy!" "Hey there, Tank!" "Scooter looks like he's been digging in the garbage again." There were rules and a pecking order among these beasts that was possibly more intricate than those governing their master's world. Several of these great dogs had their official stations that were not to be entered without invitation by man or beast. Fritz, a 250-pound St. Bernard, had a daytime official residence leashed to the railing on the sidewalk in front of Tom's market right in front of the steps down to Galena St. Although Fritz always seemed to be dozing, those on the sidewalk who attempted to step over him usually received the surprise of their lives. Puppy dog turned ferocious carnivore, and it took some acrobatic moves to deny Fritz a snack of your flesh.

Then there was Tugboat, a black and white shaggy Malamute who belonged to Bobby Kendall, one of the owners/operators of the Jerome B. Wheeler public house (the Pub). Tugboat could be found on a sunny day napping on the convertible top of Kendall's Corvair, which the dog had arranged into a comfortable nest of tattered canvas. Upon command or by his own volition, Tugboat would periodically cruise downstairs to the bar and hop up on a vacant stool. He would be poured a draft which he would carefully drink, with a lot less fuss or slobbering than most of the regular patrons.

Shadow, the black Great Dane from Chip's leather shop was like his name, a fast-moving shadow cutting through town sticking close to the buildings, keeping to himself. Buster, a husky-shepherd mix, was perpetually horny and too indiscriminate to care whether or not a bitch was in heat; if unleashed, he'd mount the first dog in sight, male or female, and start humping frantically. One half-mangled ear bore testimonial to the consequences of Buster's misguided lust. The dogs were an eclectic bunch: shepherds, huskies, malamutes, lab mixes,

Australian sheepdogs, even a large black standard poodle from Memphis named Martin. Dog fights were an everyday occurrence and the toughness of one's dog was to some a reassurance of manhood. Cruising through town on foot or with their owners on bicycles in the summer, the dogs would be greeted and talked to as though they were people, which I'm sure most of them thought they were.

At the ranch it had always been a contest to see whose dog was the gamest, most athletic of the lot. Despite the gnashing, wrestling and fighting that went on daily, the amount of serious damage was negligible until the arrival of a few Akitas, a breed known for regarding other dogs as prey. Kev Kelley's big Akita Goony literally tore the guts out of a neighbor's pugnacious bulldog, and Kev was sued to the tune of several thousand dollars (the parties eventually settled). Even the senior citizens had dogs, such as the two gigantic black dogs that were straining and snapping at everything that breathed as they rode in the back of the open jeep of their owner, Roby Albry, a veteran of the French Resistance. Having a good dog could carry more local meaning than a banker's reference sheet. "Oh, you're Gringo's dad. I know him, he plays with my pup, so you must be all right."

Now that I was living in town proper, in a succession of apartments, duplexes, shared houses etc. and had my dog Pablo, with me, I was finally accepted as a real "Local", though I still was scrambling for work, hustling as many girls as possible, and not really part of the "in" crowd, those with the good paying stable jobs and the trophy old ladies. Still, I felt that I was getting a grip on what the town and culture was really about, and I was definitely starting to have lots of fun. There still was a pecking order as I was discovering, and it seemed like there were several layers of localism. There was a distinct gap between those of us that were just hanging on, making do with old vehicles, old bicycles, old skis, hamburgers, beer and Mexican weed and those with the big houses, new trucks, Chateaubriand and good Bordeaux. A big gap. And so, just as I was becoming comfortable as an accepted local, of course the next level was looking better and I knew I could not be satisfied without getting there. It sometimes seems silly that when we finally have that which was all we thought we wanted, now we see something else that we know we must have instead. So I guess there is still no stopping.

So what is the right
for which you fight
that you think is so tight
that gives you the fright
and what of the light
that comes in the night
do you pack up in flight
or reach for new heights

CHAPTER 5:

Changing Jobs, Changing Women
and Seeing a Heavy Cash Flow

I had a bartender job in December 1971 at the House of Lum, the Chinese restaurant that moved into the basement space formerly housing Strombergs, which had moved to Larimer Square in Denver. This was a stone-walled large cavern like restaurant, and even with its stage and piano bar, was still not one of the premium bar gigs in town. Not a lot of money or action, but Greta Lum and her partner Gordon Forbes were very nice people who treated all the help well and it was a nice little family, including an exotic woman receptionist named Kaiulani, who was a mixture of Hawaiian, black, and possibly some Asian, close to six feet tall and strikingly beautiful. One night while drinking at the Pub, I somehow got together with Lori, a great looking rich girl from Chicago, who was ABC Dan's live-in girlfriend. Lori was very sensual, with large breasts and a very intelligent, fun girl. We had a real strong mutual attraction, and were soon over at her big house (while I guess Dan was out of town) getting high and having incredible sex. As she and Dan were in the process of building her big house out in White Horse Springs, near Woody Creek on a prime five acre plot, and Dan was kind of a wild guy, I thought there could be some big trouble on the horizon.

Au Contraire. In what was to be for me a lesson in grace and gentility, not only was I never threatened, but Dan was leaving his bartender job at the Mother Lode and passed the position on to me. I couldn't believe my good fortune. First I ended up with a hot, bright, sexy girl, and then the best local bar job in town. I was in a good spot, and life was getting comfortable. Also now, what I had once not understood and likened with sleazy like heroin, cocaine was presented by Lori as chic, the designer drug, not a heavy drug, but just more fun party. And we were into it, at about the same time the rest of the town was too. There would be lines in the bathrooms, toots in the little bottles, and for the "in" crowd that I was now a part of, the little carved ivory pineapple bottles of toot. The pineapple was like the even more exclusive badge, and the contents of one were only the best, the pure Peruvian, the "mother of pearl". At my bar job, it was easy to kneel down on the floor behind the bar to adjust the sound system, and have a couple snorts, then get up and serve some drinks, nobody the wiser. After I'd closed the bar, locked up and hit the street, I was wound up and ready for anything. And anything and everything was the usual in the little mining town, where several hundred locals and several thousand tourists were doing exactly the same thing. The buzz was a roar, the vibe was totally over the edge, and we were all going for it.

After camping at Lori's friend Elke's house for a month or so, Lori and I rented a house out by the cemetery and moved in together. We got along really well and really cared for each other, although in my ignorance or naivete or whatever, I was uncomfortable about the house she was building and I think I was somehow afraid of being a rich girl's kept boy toy or something like that. But things were going along okay until I came down one night with a sudden flu, huge fever, sick as a dog, just knocked off my feet. And I don't know how, but I ended up at the house of Kaiulani, the exotic creature from the House of Lum. And after she sweated out my fever, she walked on my back, gave me some kind of Hawaiian massage, sucked my toes and everything else, and made me forget all about my rich little girlfriend with a vengeance. I had a spell on me, I don't know what kind of magic this was, but it was powerful. I didn't surface for a week, and my life was in shambles, and I had a new residence. For a little guy from Ohio, I was way out of my league, I didn't even know what league I was in, but I sure knew what a fancy blow job was.

So I had really kicked Lori to the curb, just kind of ditched her. She was not the kind of girl who was accustomed to anything close to this kind of treatment, and I'm sure I had hurt her pretty badly. Which was one of the worst things I had ever done, as she in no way deserved this, being a genuinely sweet person. And bad as I felt afterward the damage had been done, there was no going back, so I just kept working at the Lode and kept on doing the do.

The Mother Lode was located in the historic old dining hall from the silver mining days and had been opened in 1966 by Gerald Williams and Harvey Rose, two very mellow individuals from Laguna Beach, CA. They started out serving inexpensive plates of spaghetti, at $2.50 affordable for everyone.

They would also feed hippies or people who didn't have money out the back door, sometimes receiving some work in exchange, sometimes not. By 1971 the Lode was one of the busiest and most popular places in town, known as a "locals" hangout. The bar/lounge area was always packed, which boasted about ten bar stools, a row of bench couches in the window and two low cocktail tables. At the time I began working there, the menu had expanded, while still being moderately priced, and the place was always bustling. The bar clientele was regular and most nights there was a standing crowd waiting for turns at a bar stool. Working there was a picnic, probably the best restaurant job possible in the town. I had my own sound system behind the bar and kept the place rocking with the Stones, Al Green, Van Morrison, Curtis Mayfield, Dr. John and all the other hot sounds. All the crazies hung out there. I had a liars poker game going most nights with 5-10 players involved, and people three deep at the bar. Usually, we were so busy that if someone I didn't know needed a drink, that person had to sit in the lounge or stand and wait for my cocktail waitress. Everyone came to the Lode and many dope missions and half-baked con schemes began there. Besides good shift pay, outrageous tips, and free food and drink, I was allowed to close early (midnight) to avoid the late night drunks and be able to get to the ski mountain first thing in the morning every day. Not to mention the fact that every girl in town came in and bartenders traditionally had pick of the litter. Talk about fringe benefits.

Now that I had been in town for a couple of years and had the good bartending job in the Lode, I was a real local, part of the scene. It seemed like I knew everyone in town, and they all knew me. There were always plenty of willing girls, sometimes two or three hanging around the bar near closing, looking to party. Sometimes this could be embarrassing, having to pick one for the night and send the others off, trying not to be rude, or piss anyone off, lest they wouldn't be there on a slower night. Rough kind of problems. But it felt good, not ego trip good, but just nice to be recognized. And with what was going on in the world, Viet Nam and all, our lifestyle seemed somehow justified, a better alternative. As for the drugs, compared to what the legal tobacco and liquor companies were pushing, we had nothing to feel guilty about. And yes, we knew that we were being lied to by our government about just about everything, so why should we swallow more lies about our drugs, which for the most part our experiences had proved not to be so harmful. When you could get up in the winter to a bright sunny day with fresh powder snow on a fantastic ski mountain, ski all day, shower, dress and work in a restaurant for a few hours, party with some of the most fun people in the world, crash out, wake up and do it all over again, who could argue? So yeah, I was feeling pretty good about here and never even dreamed about thinking of the future or family or retirement or anything remotely like that. Dumb happy, you bet. One of the waitresses at the pub was a well-built girl named Nancy Blue, with long blond hair and a great attitude. She was always upbeat and loved a good joke. Nancy had a little house on King St. in the Green Acres part of town that she shared with her Australian sheepdog, Billy. Billy went everywhere in the

Nissan Patrol jeep with her, and they were a delightful pair. She and I spent a few weeks together and had a great time.

After a while, we drifted apart, for no reason, really, but we always remained great friends. It was very sad the day Nancy overdosed on heroin. I had no idea she had ever been into that stuff. Though she hadn't been Irish, we held an old-fashioned wake for her at the Mother Lode, complete with lots of whiskey, drinking songs, and more than a few tearful tributes to a much-loved lady. But nobody even mentioned the H-word. As far as we were concerned, smack was still a ghetto drug, too low-rent and too lethal for the Aspen scene. Nancy's fatal OD was a tragic anomaly a thousand miles removed from our own benign drug habits.

When Nancy Blue overdosed and died, it hit me like a ton of bricks. I had just spent a couple of weeks with her, sleeping together, hanging out and even taking Werner Erhart's week-long Est course together, ten hours per day, every day. And throughout this whole period, we had never done any heavy drugs, (I was never into needles, never shot up once) and Nancy never mentioned her using, or showed any symptoms or any cravings.

Then, all of a sudden, she's gone. I'm not sure where I was when it happened, but I don't think I was even in town. I thought I knew this person, but I guess I really had no idea at all what she was really into. And I was a guy who thought he knew what was going on. So it hurt me on a couple of different levels, first the loss because she was really a sweet girl. Then my little ego took a hit because some part of me could not avoid the fact that I didn't know as much as I thought I did. Then there was the guy she had been partying with, who was also a good guy and one of my buddies. I wanted to blame him for it, and my mind worked hard on this one, but I ended up with, if this was his fault, then how much blame was I due as a result of my own nefarious activities. I mean, you just had to change the particular substance, and how much of the story remains the same? This type of thought pattern was very uncomfortable, and led to much doubt and self examination about what I was really doing. I had to wonder if the lifestyle was really as innocent as we liked to believe.

One of our favored modes of chemical transformation was known as the lick, or the lick bag. We called it mescaline, or vitamin m, but in reality I suppose it could have been mda, mmda, or some other chemical permutation. It was without question a fairly strong psychotropic substance. It came in the form of a brown or purple powder, not unlike Kool-aid, possibly even Kool-aid laced with the active ingredient. You could either put it in gelatin caps and ingest by swallowing, or simply use the lick bag. This seemed to be the method for instant partying. You would just wet your finger, stick it into the bag, and lick it off. This would be going on in bars, restaurants, on the ski hill, wherever: it was easy, fast, and effective. Determining the dosage was somewhat of a guess, but if you made sure to err on the strong side, you would always get off. And of course it was an easy matter to just have another lick, and another, until you were deep into the Twilight Zone. The high would come fairly rapidly, giving you a warm kinetic-energy feeling. Soon your mind would be racing, the world in slow-motion, with colors intense and brilliant, lights flashing, sounds magnified, smells delicious, and a general euphoria. You loved everyone and everything. For skiing, this "tweakly" was called the vitamin M, because it also incited boundless energy. You felt like Superman; any feat seemed possible, and mostly was. Another "benefit" was an increased capacity to drink. You just didn't get drunk -- no staggering, no slurring of words, maybe just an increase in vocal volume. If someone became offended by the partiers or was not having any fun, that person could just take a couple of licks, have a beer, and in a few minutes be roaring away with the rest of the revelers. Parties would start out with a dinner of a few people, followed by bar-hopping around town, building up numbers and momentum. By midnight or so there would be a full-fledged mob on a mission, drinking, cutting up, laughing like an asylum crew, just over-the-top funhogs. A roving riot maybe 50-80 strong with one single-minded fury: party. For observers, it was like watching a massive cartoon parade where you knew personally all the 'toons, and you could either be left out and disgusted, or have a couple licks and tag along. Welcome one, welcome all, strength in numbers, everyone loves a good party.

Among recognized holidays, the biggies

were Halloween and Fourth of July. Imagine taking a seven-day-a-week party town full of crazies, and giving them a legitimate party holiday. And in the case of Halloween, throw in the idea of universal disguises, and you've got a serious recipe for running amuck. And we certainly did. Once a guy came as an airplane, his arms taped outward to stiff cardboard wings; he had to be "fed" his booze and dope by a fellow reveler, and his "wings" proved a hazard to anyone within a four-foot radius. Among the wilder chicks, the low-cost costume of a horseless Lady Godiva was popular year in and out, though once Steffi McCarty did show up, buck-naked, astride a feisty Arab gelding who ended up rearing and tossing her harmlessly onto a couple fucking under a blanket. Talk about three being a crowd.

The party could last all day and all night. There never was any trouble; everyone was having too much fun not to get along. The recovery, though, was a different matter entirely. After being so wound up, and so alcoholled out for such an extended period, the body finally had to regroup. It was at least a two-day process to get over the exhaustion, physical pain, and mental misery. You would be so spaced out that it was hard to even know what you were doing, much less what you had done the night before. And usually your entire face would hurt from too much laughing. But the consequences were, by and large, temporary and minor. For those who want to see getting wasted as a moral issue, I would have advised them to get hold of some good weed and chill out. One night one of the gang, Sal Peachton, a high-spirited ski shop owner from back east, got too hammered and passed out in the Lode. His pals, including the owners, thought this a wonderful opportunity, and bedded him down in the kitchen, covered with mayonnaise, mustard, ketchup, salad, even pots and pans. Then they locked the place up and went home, having a great laugh. Of course, Sam was not about to let them have the last laugh. Upon waking, he showered, put on a clean kitchen uniform, and prepared himself a huge breakfast, using everything he could put his hands on and making as big a mess of the kitchen as possible. When Gerald came in to open up the next morning he found the "victim" eating like a king, half looped on Bloody Marys, with the Stones jacked up to about 11.

There were usually several dogs hanging around out front of the Lode, some inside like my Pablo who would lie at the end of the bar while I worked much of the time. This was not viewed as very remarkable back then and seldom posed a problem, save for the occasional dogfight in the lounge. A few spilled drinks, some noise and the dogs kicked out for a while. Life goes on. At closing time, while I stocked the bar, if I knew everyone there, I would lock the door and we would have a private party. This had been policy forever. Many doobies were burned in the back parking lot and many strange substances chopped up in the restrooms. I never quite got used to the look on tourists' faces when after waiting in line for the mens' restroom, the door would be unlocked and half a dozen burly locals would come spilling out, all lit up and going ninety miles an hour. What the "turkeys" thought was beyond me, especially when a whole crew would stagger out of the ladies room, along with a couple of the local babes. Whatever they thought or didn't think, there were never any incidents or complaints and the party just rolled on.

This was 1972, I was 26 and we had been through a lot of changes in this country. Two years past, there was the tragedy at my alma mater, Kent State. We had the FBI, CIA, SLA, NAACP, SLF, SDS, and God knows how many other letter named outfits, along with the major political parties, the mob, Jimmy Hoffa, the Black Panthers, and lots of hippies. There were armed camps, peace, love communes, ashrams, Hells Angels, and hare krishnas. It was like we were all searching for something, sometimes the same thing from different angles, and something quite opposite things, which brought conflicts. We had Viet Nam raging, and many of us did not buy into the government rationale, and knew somehow that the story we were being told about the war was wrong. We had Led Zeppelin, Wilson Pickett, Sam and Dave, The Temptations, Elton John, The Stones, Jimi Hendrix, The Doobie Brothers, Tina Turner, and so many more. We had Richard Nixon, and we knew we were in trouble. We also wanted answers, and they were not so easy to come by. We knew we were being lied to about just about everything, and revolution was in the air. When we smoked pot we knew that we were relaxed, peaceful and creative, and did not believe the official line about the dangers of drugs, as we had already experienced something quite different, so we knew we were being lied to. So sitting in Aspen at the end of the valley, snowed in all winter, with our own little world with our own little society, our own codes of ethics seemed a lot more realistic and honest than what was going on out there. We were skiing, partying, trying not to abuse each other except by mutual consent, and it was a better way. It was like the whole rest of the world had gone crazy and we were the only sane place left, safely hidden away in the mountains at 8000 ft, out of the fray.

Several of us had managed to acquire old Cadillacs that we used for "town cars" to cruise around town, and some of them I'm sure were incapable of cruising out of town. There were some classic beaters, from Wingbat's baby blue 59 convertible held together with bailing wire and silver tape, with not one straight piece of metal on it, but ready to start and drive any time. I had found a very clean white 60 convertible that was owned by a guy who had gone bust and was heading back to California. I heard about the car and luckily got there about a half hour before the Wingbat or I never would have gotten the car. I had to give the guy $75 cash, some Marker rotomat ski bindings, and a lid of Mexican weed and drove off in a creampuff that I used for a driver for years, eventually trading it for a Porsche 356 b coupe. The back plastic window in the top was gone, thereby making a perfect entrance over the trunk for my dog Pablo, who kept a bag of kibble in the back seat and thus had himself a very nice mobile doghouse that was always accessible no matter where I was or what I was doing. Life was good and there was always lots of fun to be had.

I suppose when you're young and dumb you don't always realize how good you have it. That certainly was the case at this time with me. Here I was, well-paid and with the best lifestyle imaginable, yet I grew bored, unsatisfied, and felt a need for more adventure.

The fast money being hauled in by the scammers was too attractive for me to ignore. At the bar I heard about people going south to Mexico, scoring weed and bringing it back, making lots of cash. Everyone smoked pot, which was obviously not harmful; legal or moral considerations never came up. Countless loads rolled through town and it was regular business to middle to friends from other parts of the country. Most everyone seemed to be involved on some level, from dishwashers and ski instructors to lawyers and real estate brokers. Everybody in the country who was moving around, traveling, skiing or partying seemed to come through Aspen at one time or another. Many would simply load up and head back home, paying for their trip and even creating some major income.

Being at the Lode most nights put me in touch with just about everyone who was scamming ("working") right in the middle of the mix. Since I was obviously not a policeman or narc I was aware of lots of activity all over the country, since people would return to town from their little missions and usually head straight to the Lode for drinks and food. There were groups from Chicago, Miami, New York, L.A., Boulder, and all points in between. Several organizations said they had moved "down-valley" to Carbondale or over to Crested Butte to achieve more privacy and lower their visibility. Some of these people would bring in boatloads of pot first from Mexico; then Columbian gold became the commercial product of choice, all but turning Miami for a time into an Aspen suburb. At the bar I heard many stories about big sailboats or trawlers loaded to the gills offloading all up and down the east coast. Also, the Columbians would send freighters and the local Florida boys would send speedboats and sport fishers out to rendezvous with the freighters, get loaded up and head for shore and the hundreds of inlets, lakes, canals and marinas where the cargo could be transferred to trucks and headed north to the cities. Since I was trusted, they told me of these exploits. Most everything was either totally "fronted" or loaded with some kind of deposit, the balance to be paid upon sale, usually within some arbitrary time frame. It was known that it was a bad idea to cheat the Columbians, with some bloody outcomes for the few that tried. This trade created many pot millionaires, many of whom would be in town with fancy new trucks, pockets of hundred dollar bills, new skis and outfits. The chairlift became known as the office, and many deals were struck there, away from prying eyes and listening ears. At some point it became easy to arrange a middle between someone who was looking for a load of product with the person who had a load. There became a complete infrastructure of folks who were supported by taking the "nickel" drive across town for $5/lb. difference in the two. A nickel on a truckload was worth $5,000 cash and sometimes could be handled in an hour or less, with virtually no risk. Small wonder why this was an attractive endeavor. There were also many opportunities for drivers, someone to move a truckload from town to a city somewhere, usually for $10/lb. or thereabouts plus expenses. The only requirements for this work were a drivers license and a certain amount of nerve. The losses suffered from this kind of transport were surprisingly small.

However, there were some spectacular incidents from time to time, now in 1972. In one such event, one of the Colorado groups had come up with a particularly daring plan. They had loaded a DC6 cargo plane in Columbia with about 30,000 pounds of Columbian and flown low into the U.S. way up to Kansas, the last place being watched for smuggling activity. They had a remote unused landing strip located, trucks at either end to turn on headlights for landing and a tanker truck to refuel the airplane and then haul away the weed in the specially constructed tank after it was emptied. This was a particularly ingenious plan and would have worked like a charm, had not one of the truck drivers taken too many Quaaludes and passed out, thereby leaving the landing strip unmarked. For the pilot coming to the end of a long stressful flight, low on fuel, in the dead of night with no place to put down, there was probably some degree of panic. In order not to crash, he exercised his only survival option, and landed on Interstate 70. In spite of losing the airplane, most of the load, and accruing large legal fees for several people apprehended at the scene, they reportedly got away with enough product before the authorities arrived to still clear one million U.S. dollars on the endeavor. I was told of this scam by the brother of the tanker truck driver who along with two or three others received one-year jail terms, and there was much speculation as to whether the one driver really took too many 'ludes or was actually an informer for the DEA. I don't think this question was ever answered satisfactorily. There were several fistfights about this controversy, with nothing definitive ever decided. The incident made the national news, and although those arrested were pressured mightily, none talked and the ringleaders were never implicated.

The amounts of money involved were staggering. In Columbia, loads were purchased for $25-30\lb. and shipped. In this country, the wholesale value was $250-300\lb. For the boat or large aircraft that was hauling maybe 30,000 pounds, the amount of cash generated was enormous. This was serious business with some serious fortunes being created.

There were the Brotherhood, the cowboy mafia, the hippie mafia, and numerous other groups operating and the whole picture was really kind of wild. There were guys out of town for a couple of months, returning and buying large custom homes and ranches, businesses, and all kinds of vehicles and toys. The scammers were not stigmatized, looked down upon or even resented by locals who weren't involved in the trade. On the contrary, they were almost folk heroes, not only tolerated but somewhat glorified. They got the best tables in restaurants, comped drinks, and people barely acquainted with the big-time dealers took pride in addressing them by their first names. Inevitably, several law firms sprang up that specialized in the kind of business that the rare but ever-increasing amount of busts demanded, with some lawyers becoming owners or partners in a varied inventory of enterprises. But there were relatively few arrests, and when they did occur, the cases were either won on procedural issues, or the sentences were rather light. After all, it was only pot.

Way up on Aspen Mountain at around 10,000 feet on the back side from the ski area is one of the old, deserted mining camps from the silver boom days of the 1890's known as Little Annie basin. Here, amid the old mine shafts and tailings are several old cabins and remains of the same. These became the home of a small group of hippies, who moved in one summer and made the place their full-time residence. Dominic, Jim Less, and Burky and their ladies had a small colony of sorts all to themselves in this spectacular little part of God's country, although without plumbing or electricity. Every couple of days, they would hike down to town to shower and do laundry at friends' houses. Since the area is accessible only by strong four-wheel drive vehicles, they had many two-hour climbs home, being without four-wheel or any kind of drive vehicle at all. Theirs was a meager existence supported only by Dominic's $8\gram hashish sales and the occasional sheet of three-eyed-toad blotter acid business. The place was idyllic, with much partying, horseshoes, scree-jumping, and the annual "Mota Movers Local 101" spring picnic.

For a while, at least, the hippies of Little Annie Basin embodied the innocence of these times, somewhat touching in their simplicity.

All this was to change rapidly and dramatically into big boats, houses, new trucks, Lear jets and the like with the arrival in town from Arizona of a Les with a purloined load of bricks of Mexican weed looking for a safe home. Les disappeared shortly thereafter, but the weed didn't, and in a blink the Little Annie hippies became Rosie and Jaime Menos, with close to a million bucks worth of product. This product was gratefully disseminated by many of the townsfolk to all parts of the country with the balance of cash bankrolling a major operation that loaded many boats and planes in Columbia with both weed and coke.

One night when I was working at the Lode bar, one of the regulars mentioned that his brother was in town from Minneapolis and needed to find 100 pounds of weed, and asked me if I could help. Having been aware of the Little Annie bonanza, I said I'd check into it; maybe I knew someone. Then there was my other old friend from Chicago, Ron Morgan, who was always looking for something to take back home, and so a plan seemed to form. I teamed up with Donny (a local stone mason supplier

and coach of our Pub softball team) who also
had a couple of customers, and we devised an
operation that would service all four customers
at the same time with a minimum of confusion
and very short exposure time for us. We had
moved all four orders down the jeep road from
Little Annie and concealed them in a little gully
near a switchback near the bottom of the dirt
road, just off the Castle Creek paved road. Then
we had all four groups run their rigs up past the
switchback and turn around and come back
down, at fifteen-minute intervals so they
wouldn't bump into each other. When they got
to the switchback, we would come out of the
brush with big duffle bags of weed, toss these
into their trucks, collect the money, send them
on their way, and move back into position for
the next group. This came off like clockwork,
and when we were through there was only to
take our jeep with the money back up to Little
Annie, pay our bill and head back to town to
divide the spoils. It was exhilaratingly easy
money, and encouraged us all to do more of the
same. Although this was a relatively modest
enterprise for myself, for the Little Annie gang

it was the beginning of a very large one. Although, I didn't realize it at the time, this relatively small transaction, which netted me a couple thousand bucks, was actually a relatively major incident for my life. Here all at once I had moved easily and profitably from the ranks of casual user and sharer to those of the well paid professional trafficker. Even though at the time I failed to recognize this significance, I had become a changed person. Without acknowledging the difference, I was now with a new mind set, and any moral considerations about this new status would just have to wait. The change was so immediate, seamless, even insidious that I just never thought about it in those terms. But for sure I now had some different thought processes going on, for I had been rewarded instantly and substantially and it would become hard to ever stop.

The "hippies" took their windfall and headed south of the border to invest in boats, and developed their relationship with Hector, a Columbian who had been living in town, skiing and partying. After sending their own boat with a couple loads into Florida and then up the east coast, Rosie and Jaime Menos began to load boats for some of the other groups to haul. As stated, the numbers for this activity were phenomenal. With boats bringing 2,000-30,000 pounds, even after paying for expenses, crew, etc., the rewards were certainly nothing to sneeze about. And as the drugs became harder, more cocaine, it seemed the people became harder also. There were more serious beefs about money, the violence began creeping into the picture, the little ski resort started being a cold nasty place. You could see the edge on people's faces, watch it in their mannerisms, hear it in their sharpness of voice. We all turned into calculating assholes, seemingly overnight. To my way of thinking at this time, as long as I had a good stash of buds, a pocket full of hundred dollar bills, a full bottle of blow, and a good looking babe to play with, good skis and plenty of cold Heinekins, life was complete. Next we needed new trucks, Mercedeses, a boat, and a Lear jet to ride on. The sick thing about it all was the attitude that we seemed to have that we deserved all of it, that it was our God–given right, because we had the balls to do what we did. It got so that if you were going down the road and you didn't have a load of weed in the truck, or a few kilos, you kind of felt naked, like you weren't doing anything. And the briefcases full of hundreds, with the load tally sheets, who had how much, who had paid how much, what was still out, how much still had to be paid to the South Americans, it all got to be a crazy blur. And the attitudes, the egos, were out of control.

We thought we were invincible, Superman, don't fuck with us, we're big, we're packin, and we sure don't mind kickin' some ass. And the whole world seemed to feed into it, as long as there were some bumps to lay out, a joint to pass, a hundred to slap on the bar, you were god, at least nobody was telling you you weren't. And when you would wake up in the middle of the night in a cold sweat with the shakes and the certain knowledge that a swat team was just on the other side of the door getting ready to kick it in, you just had to deal with it. I guess that for all the fun and good sex and partying, the tough thing was waking up in that cold sweat and realizing that we really weren't cool, that we would all go down, that we had really turned into a bunch of obnoxious selfish assholes, who were a menace, and lucky that any of us survived at all. We had not really grown into very nice people.   After we closed the Lode, it was time to cruise the Gallery to find the night's love, stash, party or all of the above.   This was a small mountain town at the end of a dead-end valley in winter, barely accessible from two directions for part of the summer, comprised of 40 or 50 bars and restaurants to handle the tourist trade.   This combination of several hundred workers along with many idle rich and many idle poor made up the Aspen version of café society, with most of the town high on something most of the time. What a wonderful and crazy life it was, with everyone loaded and fucking everyone else at one time or another; every week or so the command seemed to be "rotate."   It was like a decadent barn-dance, no fiddle or caller necessary.   There were fewer hard feelings than one would expect, probably due to the overabundance of attractive, willing players and the pleasant emotional haze of good dope.   A time of adrenaline, high spirits, and no-guilt attitudes, and it was 24\7 hard charging.

We inhibit the illicit solicit

But don't prohibit

Death habit

Terbacky habit

Death habit

Alky habit

We inhibit the cash habit

Love habit

We all inhabit

CHAPTER 6:

Moving Some Weed,
Coast to Coast Travelling

So the winter of 71-72 wound down and town mostly emptied out again for a while, but after a few weeks closing for remodeling which Gerald did every year, by middle of May or so the Lode opened up again. Which meant that I had a good bartending job, so this summer was finally going to be a lot better than the hardscrabble scratching that I had gone through the last couple years. And now I was open to scamming, shuffling weed whenever the opportunities came up, as I had a good night job, a stable income and all day to play. I had rented a little two bedroom duplex over in the Green acres connected to Wingbat's place and was now a full-fledged local, in the in, pretty much finding out in the bar about everything going on. Life was pretty good, lots of girls, lots of doobies, toot now and then, working nights, and playing some tennis during the day. I was just kind of relaxing into the pace of the town, enjoying myself, feeling good, having fun, not worrying about much at all. I seemed to have a succession of girlfriends, usually for a few weeks, then another even cuter one would be there, no hang-ups, everything real casual. Then one of the favorite summer cross-training sports became two-man volleyball, brought to town by some of the transplanted California surfer skiers. This is a fast game, good for the ski legs, that at first was played on the grass at Wagner Park in the center of town. Soon there was a fairly large playing contingent that had become hooked on the game, and somehow down near the end of Hopkins Street in a vacant lot next to Jones's house a sand court was installed, along with horseshoe pits to occupy you while waiting for your game. Jones, a local waiter/chef/restaurateur/scammer, also thoughtfully put a commercial cooler outside the side of the house so we always had plenty of cold beer. Most summer days, beginning about 11 o'clock or noon, there would be a group assemble for the day's play, two man teams, winners hold court. This would go until dark most nights, like a private club, with drink, smoke and overall good times. These games were usually fierce, but with rarely any serious disagreements. An exception occurred unexpectedly one day, however, when Jones's 'cross- the-street neighbor, Heinz Grist, drove by in his 1946 WWII Dodge Power Wagon pickup. All of a sudden, Jim Weaks, playing a game, stopped and ran out to the street yelling at Heinz, "Fuck you! Get out of that truck!" This seemed out of character for Jim, an easygoing Southern Californian, a waiter\skier about 6'3". Grist was in his sixties, a real estate broker, part of the "Nazi contingent," a rather slight fellow. Not the sort you would fairly pick a fight with.

Several of us cut Jim off. "Hey man, what's up, what the hell are you doing?"

"I was driving in town earlier and the Nazi SOB cut me off then flipped me off. He almost ran me off the road!" Weaks said.

"Forget it, we're in the middle of a game," we said as Heinz drove on down the road. So we played on for a while, everyone forgetting the incident. However, a few minutes later Heinz returned, quietly sliding his truck to a stop. He got out wearing a steel hard hat and brandishing a crowbar, and stormed onto the court yelling in his thick German accent, "Ja, Ja, now I will fight you! Let's go!" I had been his neighbor for a while the year before and worked for his partner, another Heinz, for a time; as I knew him some, I was able to cut him off and maneuver him back to his rig without any damage to anyone. The incident startled everyone, especially Jim, who was quaking in the sand, big as he was. His big mouth had suddenly turned marshmallow.

That house was the site of a couple of other strange, even darker incidents. One day, Jones and his roommate, Tim Chaz, a part-owner of Pinocchio's Pizza parlor and a charter local partier, told me they came home from an outing to find Henry Betts in the process of stealing their dirt bikes and trying to load them into his truck. They shouted him off the property and let it go at that. A very short time later, Henry was flying his hang-glider off the mountain, hit a power line, and burned off both hands up to the elbows. From then on he was known as Henry Hooks. Aspen karma, maybe, but way in excess of the abortive theft. Sadly, Chaz, one of the original good timers, OD'd on a combination of booze, coke, and Quaaludes, and died in his room one night not long after Henry lost his arms. Aspen bite. It began as a normal, raucous night at the Lode bar, with the stools full of regulars. The Nubbins brothers, Terry and Tim; big Teddy, one of the cooks; Billy, the dope lawyer; Katie Price, nicknamed "tits" 'cause she had them; Donny the Coach; Hedford, and others. At the end of the bar was Dusty Street, sitting with a rubber alligator about a foot tall, buying beers for the alligator and himself; Hunter Thompson (of *Fear and Loathing* fame) who was one of Dusty's good buddies; Weaks, Looney, and several other regulars. A normal crazy night.

A would-be badass dude came in and started hitting on Katie. "Hey tits, you wanna get laid?"

Katie didn't miss a beat. "No thanks, but my brother does -- why don't you go get your mom?"

Everybody cracked up. Then Billy chimed in. "Get your hands off her," pause, "You don't know where she's been."

So it went, back and forth, on and on, and the crowd kept slamming shots and beers and making those trips to the bathroom for a snort or the parking lot for a smoke. At one point, Donny slipped me a joint over the bar wrapped in a cocktail napkin and said, "Hey man, take a break. You gotta try this one." A few minutes later I slipped out back for my little respite. After about three hits I thought my head was going to come off; I mean I was boxed. Coming back to work was a joke only a stoner could appreciate. "Coach, talk to me," I managed to get out between calling seven aces in the liars poker game.

"It's gold Columbo from this kid from Miami that I met," he informed me.

"So when do I get some?"

"We can go up to his place in the morning."

Somehow I managed to finish the night, stock and clean the bar, and get closed up. The next morning Donny and I went up to Smuggler apartments and met Mark, from Miami. He wanted $30\oz. of the gold bud whether we took one or a whole pound. Nobody ever refused a quantity discount, but Mark did. Over the next week or two, between Donny and me, we bought most of what he had, and spread it out through the restaurant and of course smoked our own fair share, to say the least. When he was finally all out, Mark told me that I should come to Miami, and bring people of mine who were looking to load up, as he could supply whatever we needed. My job then was shared by one other bartender, John Carpenter, and we would cover for each other whenever one guy wanted to take a trip. As I had worked over a month straight every day, it was easy to get a week off to travel. That said, off I went to Miami with my friend Darrel, a mover from Ohio State who needed a load.

Hitting Miami was like going to another part of the cosmos. From 8000 ft. of dry climate to a water world, sea level; getting off the plane we found the smell of mildew with the heat and humidity stifling. These minor irritants were more than made up for by the availability of high-quality Colombian and the pure though sticky cocaine, all fresh off the boats. This one trip turned into a semi-regular gig with Mark and we had a very efficient system worked out. The method or drill then was relatively simple. We would take the buyer's vehicle to the stash house, load up and return it. Then collect usually half the money (the rest being "fronted") and the buyer would be on his way north. There was never a problem with any of this, although it was common to have to spend days in a motel waiting for that phone call saying that things were moving and someone was coming for a meeting. The drives cross-country could be a little nerve-wracking at times; every set of headlights in the rear-view looked like DEA; every fuel or food stop could seem like a trap. Of course, this paranoia was mostly unfounded. The incidents of a load being stopped on the road were very rare. A flat tire or mechanical breakdown was, however, a real challenge at times: just when you didn't need a helpful Highway Patrol to stop to assist. The action in Miami expanded to the point that some of the local clubs began to resemble the clubs back home in Aspen. Same people, same parties, same dope.

At one point Darrel from Ohio showed up when the load wasn't there and I went home empty. Since I had already made the introduction between Mark and him, and not being a professional, I didn't know how to "protect" my middle. Therefore, they later did who knows how much business together without me making one of my promised "dimes" ($10). I was really not very smart in the beginning, I suppose, not that I got much smarter later. But Miami was a real blast in those days, and who needed brains when you could have fun instead? We would hang out in several different clubs, a couple of them private, and there were always plenty of great-looking girls. Being a local boy, Mark had the scene wired. Coming from a wealthy family didn't hurt either. We always had plenty of weed and blow, and he kept a boat in the water for running around, out to Bimini, fishing, or whatever.

There was an older, very successful real estate developer named Ben Rathbone who was an associate of Mark's father. Rathbone had a home in Aspen and also owned the home in

Miami Beach where the Beatles had stayed, a major estate. We used to keep him in a free supply of pot which helped him with his cancer pain. He was a great guy, a former offshore ocean racer, who with his partner had built high-rises in Miami and Chicago as well as the Jockey Club in Miami.

One night I was driving Mark's sports car over to Ben's house with a stash when I got pulled over by the sheriff for speeding across the causeway. With a big bag in the trunk,I was fairly nervous, to put it mildly. I got out of the car, walked back to the cruiser where the cop was sucking on a fat stogie. When I gave him my four-year expired Colorado license he went into a W.C. Fields imitation: "Charles, Charles, I see no cause for any undue alarm, this license is only four years expired." With some strange, convoluted type of logic, I had figured when my license had expired that if I did not renew it and had no valid license, somehow that would make me extra careful and I would never get a ticket. The strategy that had worked so well for four years suddenly seemed to be a little less than brilliant. I was shitting my pants, thinking here we go. After checking the plates he kind of cluck-clucked and said, "You can go, but remember when you leave here that you're running from the law." That was it. What was that all about? I never found out, just went on to Ben's place, shot the shit with him for a while, then went back to the hotel. Weird. That next Sunday Mark, myself, and Root (the Okie cowboy who was also a friend of Mark's) went for a boat ride with Ben on the Patty Lou, 30 ft. cigarette-type deep vee with a couple of detuned race 492's, and Rolls Royce leather upholstery. A $100,000 80mph speedboat. We were going to the Jockey Club for brunch and we picked up Paul Hornung (the NFL star) en route. When we were out on the inter-coastal Ben opened her up to about 75 in a heartbeat. Root complimented him with one of his better "cornpone-isms." "Shit howdy, this sucker gets a hump in her back like a tall dog shittin' peach seeds!" We all just about fell overboard.

Miami and then back home to Aspen: that was the route. One trip I was taking back to Colorado got a little too exciting. We had some 60-80lb bales of extra potent Columbo (we used to code name it Peter Falk) and I had picked out one green one that was particularly pungent and gooey. Killer. Anyway, I was taking this one home with me, along with a girlfriend, Rita, I had hooked up with there. Since we were flying commercial, there were some logistical considerations, so to speak. I got two standard solid Samsonite large suitcases, cut the bale in half, double seal wrapped both pieces and barely managed to stuff them into the suitcases and close them. I mean they were packed; I needed to use a carry-on bag for my clothes. We got to Miami airport where I was going to just check my bags through. But it was the last minute for the flight so they wanted me to run the luggage through the x-ray right there. Instant cold sweat. I mumbled some inane excuse about being sick, emergency, grabbed everything and bolted for the door. What to do? We hopped in Rita's car and raced up to the Ft. Lauderdale airport and managed to get on a flight leaving in an hour. Checked our bags, headed to the bar, and managed to get hammered enough to get on the plane.After changing planes in Dallas\Ft. Worth and Denver we arrived at Sardy field in Aspen; of course the suitcases were not on the plane. The baggage people said there would be another flight from Dallas later that afternoon, and maybe our luggage would be on it. We hastily set up a small retrieval team, replete with three vehicles, shotguns, auto, etc., expecting the worst (not that we had any real intention of a shootout).

Actually, the conclusion of this little episode was rather anticlimactic; it involved no more than walking into the airport after the flight had arrived, spotting the suitcases sitting on the floor by the wall, picking them up and walking out the door. Big mission.

That weed was the all-time best, and it caught a lot of people's attention, including Connie Cohen, a lady from Chicago, who was a very outspoken, foulmouthed, crazy wonderful chick into everything. Connie had a "little brother," Peter Cicero, from the Chicago Heights section of the Windy City, a grandson of one of Al Capone's bodyguards. Peter Cicero was a crazy guy, the boss of his own world in Chicago. He lived with his girlfriend, Monique, his two brothers, mom and dad, and Grandma in the old family fortified mansion. Peter was an energetic hustler/dealer, a barrel of a guy, pretty much a badass. Peter wanted all of this bale to take back to Chicago. Not only that, he wanted me to hook him up with the Miami flow, as he said he had an organization that could handle large amounts regularly. This seemed like a good plan, just what I needed, a major ongoing market so that I could finally have the big flow, big income. So off we went, back down to Miami, to make the arrangements. Usually the buyers paid a substantial deposit before taking the load on the front, with the balance to be paid after everything was sold. Right from the start Peter was kind of greasy, not coming up with the cash, sneaking a load out of town that was supposed to stay put until much of it had been cashed out, so we had the Miami boys on our back right from the get- go. Anyhow, the load got to Chicago, and then there was an excruciatingly frustrating period when I would fly from Aspen to Chicago to round up cash, only to end up stalled, hanging around Connie's apartment for days at a time, waiting for Peter to show up, listening to every kind of excuse and stroke imaginable, all the while taking heat from Miami about their cash.   This was definitely not the glamorous outlaw lifestyle we were supposed to be enjoying.   Piece by piece, I would then fly from Miami to Chicago with bags of cash, sometimes picking up in Atlanta or N. Carolina also as a favor to the Miami guys.   I would usually hang in Miami for a couple of days, party, then fly back to Aspen.   Too bad I wasn't able to log my frequent flier miles.   I'd have had lots of free trips.

Life at this time seemed like a long drone of sitting in hotels and apartments, boring, boring, boring, interrupted by short missions of intensity, adrenaline and risk.   In Miami at this time there were many turf struggles being waged, with boats blowing up, houses burned, people even getting killed.   But mostly things were routine, and it was no big deal to jump in a truck or a car with 300-400 pounds in the trunk and take off.   Some groups would sell a load by turning over the keys to a sedan full, and the buyer would just drive off with the whole thing, car and all, title in the glove box, all one price.   This Chicago thing moved along for a while, albeit in fits and starts, until one day in Aspen we got a bad phone call. It seemed that Peter Cicero had OD'd on something and had been found dead at a drug lab of some sort that he had been running. Great. I flew back to Chicago and since I was a partner (though not in the drug lab), I rented a limo and took the family to a funeral ordeal for the day. This was very sad, of course, a traditional Italian rite. Mama C (Peter's grandmother, the Capone gunner's widow) was a little Sicilian lady about five feet tall, tough as nails. Throughout the whole process she didn't shed a tear, though Peter was her favorite, or say a word. Only when we were leaving the church for good did she say "Goddamm it, grandpa never did any of his own shit." Hello.

After coming back to town from all the travel and time in south Florida, the air felt crisp and the cool was restorative. But after only a few days in town, I began to notice some changes. There seemed to be a proliferation of gold chains and silk shirts where there had been cowboy boots and hippies before. The LA contingent had swelled as had the Philly and New York groups. There was even a Rolls being tooled around by Bobby Rizzo, supposedly of one of the major Philly families. About thirty, with dark-haired good looks, the word was that he was a major cocaine supplier and hit man. And on the flight in on Aspen Scareways from Denver there was a guy chatting up the stewardess who was actually wearing a gold razor blade on a gold chain. Talk about subtle. As if the new crowd wasn't enough, the whole mood seemed to be different. Things seemed tense, everyone was uptight. Where the keyword used to be mellow, now the pace was frantic, too busy, and entirely too serious. Where before there were none, now there were beefs, big disputes about who owed what and how they would cover it. At one point Steve from Miami was trying to collect for half a kilo or something and he took to stabbing the guy's little dog with a ski pole. This coldness didn't sit well in the mining town, and Steve was never liked after this.

It seemed like the whole community was involved with toot, it almost became a toot economy. I mean you couldn't party without the girls checking first to make sure you had at least a couple of grams before you came over. The parties were all-nighters, with prodigal amounts of the powder being inhaled, and whole cliques going on two or three day runners with no sleep. The amount of skiers on the mountain in the morning was reduced greatly, with most locals getting up at the crack of noon. There began a coke-based economy, with grams and eighths, quarter oz's and oz's being the currency, and in the restaurants and shops the barter system was in full swing, people trading toot for dinners, tips, wine, skis, clothes, and even automobiles. The smugglers were gods, and it seemed like suddenly, everyone was a dealer. Then there were the busts, with people from dishwashers to architects to trust-funders being apprehended with pounds and kilos.

The whole thing got completely out of hand, the town was sick, and the wealthy Hollywood crowd that were buying up all the homes for the huge prices were right in the thick of it along with everyone else. There was a paranoid, unreal atmosphere about the place that was difficult not to get caught up in, because when you were buzzing good, putting fast cash in your pocket, and having sex with lots of beautiful women, and when you woke up (if you could call a nervous cold sweat resting sleep) it only took a good wake-up bump to get you rolling and start the process all over again. And we thought we were really having fun now.

So what had seemed like a long-term pay from Chicago had ended up a big mess. So much for science. There were always new worlds to conquer, of course, one of them being L.A., since a group of ski freaks, playboys, and crazies from Beverly Hills were living in town. They thought that they could move some weed back home, so off we went. We started by me driving a pickup from Aspen out (loaded of course), a 16-hour drive cross country, very scenic but also a high anxiety kind of trip, what with 1,000 pounds in the back. Sometimes running at night I would hear all sorts of strange sounds while highballing across the desert. I'd be sure that the wheels were falling off, or that the lights behind me had been there for two hours, so of course I was being tailed. All sorts of mental terror. All I could do was burn another one, keep the hammer down and hope for the best. At one pit stop, I came out of the restaurant to find two highway patrolmen standing right by the truck gawking at my big dog lying on top of the load. Instant bullet sweat. I walked up and asked them if they'd like to meet him. "Oh, no, that's okay," they hurriedly said, "Don't do that." I tipped my baseball cap, and my guard-dog and I headed on our way.

Since Sandy and the Beverly Hills boys were local, and he had a younger sister, we had lots of young girls hanging out partying; it was really somewhat Bacchanalian. Sandy was also of the belief that it made more sense to pay a hooker $100 than to take a date out to dinner, half-gram, wine, etc., and still maybe not get the job done right. Consequently, there were always a couple of great-looking blondes around, and they provided varied entertainment for all.

The word of the day was "casual," and it applied to work as well as play. One time Mark was coming in from Miami with a small load. He had taken the red-eye to LAX, and when I picked him up at the airport all he had was a shoulder carry-on and a footlocker completely stocked with gold Columbo. We just picked it up at baggage and dragged it out to the curb. But I was driving an SL convertible that week, and the trunk was way too small for the footlocker. We just stuck it in and drove with the trunk lid up, the trunk hanging out, no big deal. We figured that if we acted like we owned the place and knew what we were doing, we wouldn't attract any attention, and we didn't.

This summer and fall of 1972 were finally over, it was winter, high season with town full of tourists, and most importantly the mountain open for skiing. What a crazy off season with all the traveling, scamming and all, it seemed like I had aged ten years in a few short months. I think I was still in some sort of shock or lingering jet lag or something, and even though I had passed a lot of cash through my hands, I hadn't really ended up with very much. It seemed like the only way to really make a big hit was by somehow having my own load. After all the excitement I was looking forward to just working the bar, partying and skiing. And much as I had become a part of the hustle, the new economy, I wasn't real comfortable with what the town was becoming.

At the Mother Lode I became friends with one of the waiters, Abe Lewis, who was known as one of the better skiers on Aspen Mountain. He agreed to let me follow him around while he gave private lessons to Lenny Hess, a friend from Chicago, an ex-Nam guy who was something of an animal. One of the other waiters got me a demo deal on a pair of the new glm Kneissl 170 cm. skis which were easier to work than the old 205 cm. Heads and I was ready to go. I think Abe appreciated me for sheer entertainment value, as I had the crazy notion that since it was only soft snow, there was no way I could get hurt, and my motto was "No Guts, No Glory". Needless to say, I took some memorable beaters. At some point, though, I got a copy of "Teach Yourself to Ski," a fantastic book written by Georges Joubert, the coach of the French ski team for years, and the developer of the modern technique that all the racers use. This book breaks it all down so it makes sense and is packed full of diagrams, photos, and drills. I dedicated myself; I would not be satisfied until I could ski with any of my friends anywhere, even though many of them had skied most of their lives.

I would take the book and a snack in my backpack, get to the mountain at opening, and take twelve runs on Bell Mountain (the steepest, most difficult, mogul laced part of the mountain) before hiking from number 6 up to Gretl's restaurant for lunch. Every lift ride I would study my book, most days skiing alone, as this was fastest. Soon I could negotiate any terrain on the mountain, usually faster than my more skilled and certainly more experienced friends. Other than Abe, whom I called coach because of his generosity with his assistance, most people seemed resentful that a mere beginner like me could beat them down the hill. I don't mean to sound smug. I just discovered that very few people really skied hard, and most were actually inhibited by a healthy amount of fear and/or laziness. At this time, the short ski controversy was quite heated although their effectiveness as a learning tool was very obvious.

Eventually, I wore out my little skis, just beat them into junk really, and moved to a 207 Rossignol, and actually was able to go much faster, which was wonderful. Now I really started to feel like I belonged.

One day I stopped at Gretl's restaurant on the mountain for a bite of lunch, I ran into

Nancy and Leslie, two of the local lovelies. Nancy's dad owned Buttermilk Mtn, and was therefore a major stockholder of the Aspen Skiing Corporation, and Leslie was from one of the leading families and of course they were both very good looking and expert skiers. This day, they had in tow Jack Nicholson, the actor, who spent a lot of time in town, bought old Judge Shaw's mansion on Hallum lake, and was a regular, good guy, accepted by the locals as one of the gang. We had lunch together with Jack cutting up, keeping us all in stitches, really a funny guy. We were a little loud, a little crude, and having a wonderful time. When we got back on the hill and put our skies on, I saw that the girls were not really helping Jack with his skiing, but instead seemed to be taking their delight watching him crash and flail down the mountain. This didn't seem real fair or funny to me (male bonding, I guess) so I stepped in and started sharing the tricks and techniques that I had so recently learned. Jack was a real go get em guy, not scared, with a great spirit, and he picked up quickly and was soon cruising pretty well. This seemed like a lot more fun to me than making fun of someone's mistakes. Jack seemed to have been enjoying himself all day anyway, but I'm sure he appreciated the slight lessening of bumps and bruises.

There was a sweet odor of bud in the air most days riding the chairlift, and many humorous tree stops. The funniest days were "vitamin" days when we'd take either a hit of acid or some mushrooms. Those days were sparkly; the snow whispered; you never got tired or even winded. On some powder days, it seemed like everyone on the mountain was lit up. Then after ski, some of the finest food and wine to be found anywhere in the world. The mountain was our country club, and the wealthiest and the poorest shared in all of the amenities. Thank you, Jesus. For the rest of the season, winter 1973, I did just as I had planned, skied, partied and worked at the Lode. It was a great year, I had actually figured out how to get around all over the mountain in one piece, crashes becoming fewer and not so painful (usually). I had hired as my cocktail waitress a gorgeous stacked blond, Stephanie, even though she had a boyfriend, Michael Pokress. Though I (along with all the other guys) was very attracted to Steph, her boyfriend was cool and we became good friends and I left her alone.

Pokey, as he was called, was a good looking dude, a waiter at Andre's, real strong and athletic, an expert skier. One of the few days that we hooked up together on the mountain led to one of my more memorable crashes. It was a brilliant March day, with the deep blue clear sky and about a foot of fresh powder, just about as good as it gets. We were cruising down all the steep bump runs, just bombing in the soft powder. After cutting up most of Bell Mountain, Silver Queen, and Aztec, we headed for the 1A liftline. Pokey took the left side and I took the right. We were hauling ass, pounding the bumps, exploding the soft snow, getting air, just going crazy. About six or seven turns down the steep tree-lined run, I hit a bump and didn't pre-jump enough and found myself launched about ten or fifteen feet off the ground, airborne for a long time, heading to the trees beside the trail. It seemed like I was in the air for an eternity, just in space, and I had a flash of seeing myself hitting a tree, going to the hospital, and wearing lots of plaster on my leg. This movie was like a blink, and then I smacked into a tree about eight feet off the ground. Since I had seen it coming, I had attempted to turn my skis and hit with my feet but I was not quite quick enough. I had gotten my left foot around, but not my right one, so I hit with my left ski and my right knee and face, just splatting and sliding to the ground in a heap.

I must have been out for a few seconds because the next thing I knew I was in a pile of gear at the bottom of a tree with the lift above me full of people screaming. I got up and though kind of dizzy and a little spaced out started shaking myself and collecting my gear, which amazingly was all there and usable, though somewhat torn up. As I looked up at the tree that I had abused I was amazed to see that it was an aspen tree with about a one foot diameter trunk that for some reason was not straight as aspens are, but had a big crook in it that looked like a big letter "c".

I cruised down the lift where Pokey was waiting and took stock of things. One of my pals, Buddy Ortega, who was a patrolman, showed up and said that he had been dispatched to a serious crash on the run but didn't see anything and asked if we had. I had to laugh kind of sheepishly and told him that it had been me and it was a pretty bad crash, but I was mostly okay. My knee was a little bit numb though, and I knew that once I quit moving on it and the shock wore off I would probably be out of action for a while. Since it had been such a spectacular day I didn't like the idea of sitting around for days not skiing, with only the memory of a crash to think about. So while I was still functional we decided to ride up 1A and number 8 (Ruthie's) then jump down Keno (out of bounds) so I could have a good powder run to think about while I was laid up. Which we did, in about three or four feet of steep untracked powder all the way down to Castle Creek road, where we had to hitch a ride back to town.

It was getting dark by the time we got back to town and I found a girlfriend at the mountain and got driven up to the hospital. They took x-rays but said I was lucky and there were no breaks, only a dented tibia right at my knee. I was hurting and spent a few days on crutches, but at least I had that last powder run to dwell on, not my wipeout. I realized that I was now hopelessly in love with a sport, and a mountain.

Looking back now it seemed incredible that almost five years had passed since I stopped playing music in order to practice so I could come back better. The time had flown past and other than booking the bands and acting as Michael's manager for a time, I had done nothing to satisfy my creative self. I had gotten so caught up in Aspen, the life, skiing, and just plain surviving that there just hadn't been time for woodshedding, I didn't even have a keyboard with me during this time. Now and then I would remember what I once had been and think about how it would be to be playing again, but something would always come up, someplace to go, something to do, and the thoughts would be left behind. Things were happening too fast and I didn't fully realize that a major part of me was being neglected.

I was living pretty well, even though I didn't really have anything to show for it other than some good memories. But even good seasons end, and soon it was Easter again, last day on the mountain, no more skiing for a half-year. This year, I packed up for the off-season and headed out to Marin County to avoid the depressing rain and mud, catch a little California sunshine, and heal up my bumps and bruises, both mental and physical.

still up to your antics
is this just semantics
always so frantic
go trans atlantic
is it automatic
a real panic
or just fantastic

CHAPTER 7:

Weed Turns to Blow, Things Get Crazy

Out in Marin County, Ca. in Mill Valley was where my drummer from Rush, Bo, was living, along with old Burt from Chicago and his old lady, Sally. They had a cool house in the hills, lots of room, and despite the incident with Burt and Sparrow, we were still friends, so there was no problem with them inviting me to come out and visit for a while. Bo was a total madcap pal from Dayton, who had played with several other groups, was also a pretty clever scammer and along with Burt was in college and business in the video industry, with some interesting projects in the works. And Sally was a real upbeat chick, about six feet tall, blond, very slender with a beautiful model face, which she was. So I just hung out with them for a couple weeks, getting what sun there was on the deck, smoking doobs, going out to dinner, partying with the local crowd they were in with, taking it easy for a change, relaxing. One night Sally and I hooked up which was great and afterward seemed kind of justified given the history between Burt and me. But not that that was the reason, not at all, Sally and I had always been attracted to each other, even way back in Chicago, and all this had nothing to do with Burt, Sparrow, or anyone else other than ourselves. Sally was very bright, a very sweet person, just a delight.

One night we went to dinner in Sausalito at a place called Valhalla, owned by Sally Stanford, the famous madam from an earlier era who was now respectable. Somehow, Burt and Bo had been involved with a video production about Sally and the place (which was on the same site as the old brothel) and so had an acquaintance with the venerable lady. She happened to be there while we had dinner, so after eating, I was introduced and was lucky enough to have a lovely conversation in the big lobby, filled with overstuffed couches, stained glass, all Victorian splendor. What an amazing person. Sally Stanford was wise, sophisticated, and gracious, seeming to have a grasp of everything, and still was very down to earth, and had a way of making everyone feel important and special. What a person. We talked for I don't know how long about seemingly everything under the sun, as if we had known each other all our lives, just a very comfortable, warm evening. I'm sure she has the same effect on everybody, that's just the way she was. This was an event from another time, somehow, totally alien from the usual high-speed hustle I managed most of the time in my life, like a breather, a glimpse of a different style, and the encounter left me feeling like I had received a very nice gift.

All too soon my break was winding down, it was time to get back to town, the restaurant would be opening for the summer, hopefully the mud had dried up some, and I was ready to travel. I was antsy, packed up, made my goodbyes, and headed back to the hill.

Back in Aspen, the party was rocking along as usual in Spring '73. One day as I was riding my bike down Hopkins Street from the volleyball court, a black Volvo pulled up beside me and flagged me down. It was Everett, a nefarious character from Chicago who had recently gotten married to blonde Betty, a beautiful, lissome thing who had worked at North Beach Leathers with my former live-in Sparrow. Everett and I had talked months previously about teaming up und going to

Mexico to bring in our own load of weed, as he felt that we could establish the same connections as the other Chicago boys had. "You gotta come up to the first cabin at Seven Castles," Everett said with no preamble. "I'll be back there in an hour. Come alone. Hurry." With that he sped off. He seemed pretty jacked up, and since he was a real loony tune, I had no idea what was up. But Betty was gorgeous, also from Chicago, some kind of heiress supposedly worth a couple million. Beautiful, wealthy, crazy, clever, and also one of the hardest, most selfish, chicks you could ever find. And not just because she wouldn't fuck me. Contrary to my studly aspirations, I had come to sad terms with the fact that some babes inexplicably found me resistible. Anyway, I cruised through town, stopped by the Epicure restaurant to pick up a sandwich and cancel my lunch meeting, then went home to drop off my bike and pick up my truck. Now, Seven Castles is about ten miles up the Frying Pan River from Basalt, past the Wooden Handle where I used to live, and is named for the seven massive red rock formations that rise up like mini-mountains, sheer steep rock faces, quite spectacular really. At the base of this formation, just off the road, are a couple of homes and a group of several cabins that were rentals. At the time, these were as remote accommodations as were available, twenty miles down-valley to Basalt, then another ten miles up the Frying Pan. Nobody ever went down there unless they had to, and nobody had to. So muttering and grousing all the way, I puttered down the road to see what my little buddy was up to. I found the cabin with the Volvo out front, knocked on the door and when Everett let me in I couldn't believe my eyes. Betty was sitting at the kitchen table with a buck knife, digging into a pile of shiny chunky white powder about two feet tall, spread out on newspapers. About twice the size of a basketball. She was taking about a 1 half-gram sized snort off the blade of the buck just as casually as smoking a cigarette. My eyeballs must have been jumping out of their sockets; this had to be a few pounds of cocaine.

Betty seemed to read my mind. "Yeah, when we got to Mexico, we couldn't hook up with anyone so we just cruised on down to La Paz, Bolivia and met some cool folks." They evidently had scored this pure stuff there on their honeymoon, then simply packed it in bags, taped them to their bodies, wore loose clothes and flew home, walking right through customs. Gulp. Of course we all proceeded to get jacked up pretty good, drank a couple cases of beer, and jabber-jawed all night. The deal was that they needed me to help unload the big pile before we snorted it all so they could head back down south to re-up. I took a big bag for samples and headed back to town to make the rounds. Toot was the prevailing item now, with a gram being the prerequisite for almost every type of activity, whether a dinner party, date, ski outing, whatever. Everyone was snorting: the restaurant crowd, ski schools, real estate magnates, lawyers, mechanics, secretaries. Everybody. It got so blatant that at one point the mayor wrote an open letter to the townspeople in the paper, begging everyone to be cool and stop doing drugs so openly; please go to the bathroom or at least somewhere out of sight, because we don't want a bunch of feds coming into town getting all of us in trouble. I still couldn't figure out what the tourists (turkeys) thought when six or seven people would get up from a table and pile into a bathroom together for 10 or 15 minutes, then come spilling out talking a mile a minute all at once. Some of us perfected what we thought was a better, less conspicuous style; we would stay at the table, put a bread plate in the middle, pour the gram on the plate, and tear open and spill several packets of sugar all around it, leaving the papers scattered around. Then you would just take your knife, make sure no one was watching, dig in and have your toot right in front of God and everyone. And no one was the wiser. Oh, we were so clever.

The Bolivian that Everett and Betty had brought was totally pure, very strong, and therefore highly desirable. It was not too difficult to find buyers and for a while I thought I was Superfly. I had the stuff all over town, people moving all the time; I had it coming out my ears. I could trade product for skis, dinners, clothes, cars, stereo's, just about everything. I don't know if it was because I had moved a few different loads of weed, or because I now thought I liked a toot here and there partying, or because everyone else was doing it", but somehow it seemed like no big deal to help move as much of this Bolivian as I could get my hands on. It was just too easy, I guess, here it was just put in my hands for a low wholesale price, all fronted, and all I had to do was break it down and unload it, for real good profit. Like I say, after the weed, and after getting used to snorting the stuff along with everyone else I knew, I never really stopped to consider any moral considerations, never thought that the stuff could be real dangerous. It was just another party favor; part of having a good time, and the town was full of really nice, interesting, good attractive people all partying so where was the harm? Even though I could have maximized profits by breaking it down into small quantities and making lots of sales, I was either too paranoid, careful, or lazy, and instead always tried to deal with fewer people who would buy larger quantities. The margins were smaller, but so was the risk. And I always said "just because you're paranoid doesn't mean there's no one after you." Calming thought. And this summer of 1973 I was working the bar at the Lode, where they would be packed four and five deep, and I would have the place liquored up and rocking to Al Green, Curtis Mayfield, Van Morrison, Dr. John, the Stones and more, just a great scene every night. And out of consideration for the owners, who were good friends, I never did any dealing from the bar. In fact even though I might have just picked up a large quantity of new product, I would ask around and kind of put the word out that I was looking to buy a gram, which I would do, even though I had a shitload in my stash. I thought I was pretty clever, establishing such good cover, nobody would ever guess that a lot of stuff was coming from me, I thought. So it was a pretty wild summer and eventually everything was gone and Everett and Betty headed back down South to reload on an even grander scale. And I just kept working, waiting for their return, not too worried, not feeling guilty, just looking forward to some cash income, maybe buying a lot or something, trying to keep pace with my peers, Aspen style. I didn't consider myself a bad guy or anything, it seemed like what I was doing made everyone happy, and though stealth was necessary to avoid trouble, I surely wasn't trying to hurt anyone, and didn't view myself as a criminal or anything. Unfortunately, the authorities of several countries did not share my views and Betty and a couple of her beautiful blond girlfriends were body-packing through Mexico when they were tripped up going through customs in Mexico City. Busted. They were to be locked up for years, Betty for more than five in a Mexican prison. Not pleasant. Everett was not caught, but he became hated in town, the villain. It was as if the Sundance Kid had blithely let Etta Place take the rap for him. One night at the Lode bar, I had to rescue Everett from a gang of the girls' friends who wanted to take him out to the dumpster, possibly limb-by-limb. Letting your old lady take the fall was bad news all the way around. The whole town was wired. The pace and the mood were getting harder, though, and some people didn't snort it; they had to inject it. Big Todd, a very gentle, affable guy, was found dead, OD'd one day. Next John Dutton OD'd, and on and on.

But most of the casualties merited no national headlines. One day, for unknown reasons, old Gloves took out his nine-millimeter and blew his brains out. People were dropping pretty fast. It was almost becoming routine, and drugs, especially toot, deadened a lot of us to the local body-count. A major bust seemed just as tragic as an OD or gun death.

During this time, the whole mood of town seemed to keep changing, as more and more, coke or toot became the in-vogue item, the measuring device, currency, the new coin of the realm. It was more than a fad; it was pervasive, what everyone was into, in one manner or other. Some people were commercially involved, from the smuggling level all the way down to the street sales level. Dial-a-gram. And it seemed that the heavier the involvement, not only the more toys and Dom Perignon but also the more respect from all quarters of the community. Where the way to get laid used to be, "Hey you wanna go burn a doobie?" now that would only draw a yawn, and maybe a little condescending pity from the local lovelies. But with "Hey, lets go do some toot," all things were possible, the only limit being the size of your bag as to how far you were going to get. Do the names "bag bitch" and "coke whore" mean anything? Girls who had been so nice, innocent and sweet were now hard, calculating trade-off artists, I often griped to myself, even as I was all too happy to play my part in these supply/demand exchanges. I wasn't the only one. You could trade a bag for skis, motorcycles, cars, drinks, dinners, sexual favors or God knows what else. As long as you had the nose candy, you were styling. And this cynical mean-spiritedness provoked a great deal more police activity, many more busts, beefs, snitches, and other trouble. The parties I went to now ended up being all-nighters, sometimes for days on end, with staggering amounts of the powder consumed. Usually after a short time, a few lines, the room would become full of geniuses, experts on the entire world, highly opinionated motormouths going at it face to face with no clue as to what anyone else was talking about, or for that matter what they were talking about themselves. So much fun, so enlightening, such a waste of time, funds, and energy. And although naked hot-tub parties were frequent, the amount of sex actually decreased dramatically for lots of folks, as many men were shocked to learn about the "cocaine shrivelies." This left many of the ladies feeling less than adequate, until some figured out how to have their fun with each other. Two women could be playing in the hot tub while the boys, oblivious, played backgammon or darts, sometimes for ridiculously high stakes. And there was the local activity of "window scratching," late at night, after hours, when you were wired and needing a woman. As long as you could find one home alone and had a big enough bag of wake-up, you could probably be invited in and "serviced," all for the price of a few good toots.

Then one day at the volleyball court something happened that could be seen as a bad sign. I was getting ready to serve, facing east, when I heard what sounded like maybe a big truck backing into a loading dock or something, a loud boom, but instead of the sound coming from the road, it was overhead. I looked up to see a two place glider begin a slow agonizing spiral from about

12,000 feet corkscrewing into the ground, someplace toward Smuggler mountain. There were no chutes, the two people just rode the thing into the ground, being killed instantly. This was like watching in slow motion, being helpless to do anything, just watching people get killed. There were many stories later, one had an unidentified jet speeding away after the sound, another had some type of bomb sabotage, but there was never anything conclusive decided. The people were two guys from Chicago who were supposedly involved in the trade to some large extent. All I know is that a very warm day turned real chilly. The coke thing just kind of exploded, changing in perception from a hard core drug for lowlifes, like heroin, to the new chic drug of the haves more than the havenots. And it was everywhere, it seemed that the whole world was being figured in oz.s, grams, quarter pounds, kilos, eightballs, teeners, and so on. And instead of the negative social stigma previously associated with it, now this was the hip condiment of the movie people, athletes, players, those on the inside. And the business was flourishing. People were getting in the middle all over the place, from all walks of life. With a good supplier and a couple of good movers for outlets, you could have a large regular supply of cash. And since this was a new toy, at first we didn't realize how addictive it could get. After partying all night, getting a couple hours sleep and trying to function, that little wake up bump became a necessity, and the cycle just started all over again. Never mind the paranoia, cold sweats, irrationality, and those amazing creatures that you would blow out of your nose every morning, marble sized technicolor clumps that couldn't be good for you. But the power of the drug was strong, and many decisions about everything were probably made just to service the jones. We were not so innocent anymore. We had traded lots of our morality and ethics for the all powerful bump. And it just seemed to happen, with no clear cut beginning and certainly no end in sight.

Just as the people and attitudes had changed, seemingly overnight, the landscape of town had also been transformed, looked different. All the streets had been paved, no gravel roads left in town, even most of the alleys had been done. On Main Street, they even put in two traffic lights, one in front of Carl's pharmacy, and one at the

Hotel Jerome. And not only that, some of the streets (Hyman between Galena and Durant, part of Hopkins had been turned into a pedestrian mall, with park benches and planters!) This was unbelievable, with some of the access streets now even one way feeding around the mall. Some of us locals were real unhappy about this development as it completely interrupted the cruising route through town in our old Caddie convertibles, and made those wheelborn pickups next to impossible. We thought it would be a good idea to head on down to Denver's Larimer Square and pick up a busload of bums, give them each a couple bottles of cheap wine, and haul them up the valley to be installed on our new park benches. Although a good plan of civic spirit, we could never get sober or serious enough at the same time to pull it off.

And on the mall itself as well as all over downtown, the quaint little shops were giving way to newer, slicker more megastores, everything bigger. Jesse Maddalone even built a large, rest stop looking Conoco station on Main Street at Galena, that was like a full service freeway facility. There were new two-and three-story condos going up all over, Aspen Square taking up a whole block, with shops on the ground floor, underground parking, the full meal deal. Most of the original funky Victorian houses were being transformed from well worn local digs to half-million-dollar period showpieces. And the monopoly players were filling up the paved streets with their shiny Benzes and you could even spot an occasional Rolls as the town seemed to be growing into Hollywood in the hills. And at Sardy Field, the Cessna 172's and Pipers were now relegated to the back forty as most weekends there was a front line filled with Lears, Citations, G3's and such, because we now had oil royalty as well as the movie variety. And with all this progress, many of us lamented the loss of our little hidden paradise in the mountains.

As the summer of days of 1973 grew shorter and the air got colder, I could see that I was living in a different town, and time no longer dragged as it had in those summers in Basalt. Now there was almost as strong a summer tourist season as the winter, there didn't seem to be much of an off-season that fall at all. There was just an amazing fast-paced energy, lots of building, lots of new people, many more people, just a whole new feel to the town, and the only constant seemed to be the mountain, the giant in our midst, always there, beautiful green in summer, brilliant white snow-covered starting in fall, under that sky so blue on a clear day, a deep deep blue almost purple or black, a thing of imposing beauty which cared nothing for drugs or no drugs, wealth or not, skiers or not, a living entity of itself, regardless.

And I was now a local for sure, part of the scene, the in-crowd or whatever, but I didn't really feel any different, a little more stable maybe, but I still knew that I wasn't finished, I thought I was on the verge of getting rich, having all the toys, buying into the whole superficial American dream, Aspen style. And for however hip I may have thought I was, I was really just another misdirected soul, buying into the current goals, not really taking time to analyze and take my own well thought out positions. But I sure had myself fooled.

She's just a coke whore
need I really say any more
she's so glad just to see you
as long as you first stopped by Peru
and you may think you're pretty smart
but she knows what you're saying before you
even start
and if the fun should hit a snag
all you need is a bigger bag
so don't blame her and don't blame me
'cause we only see what we want to see

CHAPTER 8:

Crazier still to Asia, Almost Killed Myself

With the girls in prison, and all that Bolivian action come to a halt, my big cash-flow stopped again. You might think there was a message here, but I guess I still wasn't real smart. One of Everett's friends was a sleazy character, Jerry, from New York, who contacted me and wanted to meet in person. We met at his current lady's house, a large estate on the west side, very formal, old money. Jerry had a mission planned and he wanted me to do the job. He offered $50,000 cash, which was a lot, enough to buy a lot, a truck, and have a good start towards building a house. What I had to do was take a group tour to the Far East and retrieve a couple bottles of "local liquor." Of course the bottles would just be masquerading as the local blend, and would really be filled with what I didn't want to know about. You know, pure ignorance, which I thought would make me cleaner, Right. Although I didn't feel real good about Jerry and his plan, whatever it was, business was business, and we rationalized with the notion that if not me, then someone else was going to do this anyway; after all demand was demand and people who wanted something were going to get it through one means or another. The whole thing made my skin crawl, but the $50,000 paycheck got the best of me and I agreed to go. The plan was highly organized; these were serious New York folks with God knew what type of affiliations, and they were definitely not to be trifled with. Step one, I needed a passport, and a car parked in long-term parking, at San Francisco International Airport. I went to LA, hooked up with my car dealer pals, went to the auction and picked up a Sedan de Ville for not much dough, put some shocks and tires on it and drove to SF. Got a passport in two days, while I stayed with Sally, now Burt's ex, all the while saying nothing about my plans. I had been given a travel package, a group tour to Japan, Indonesia, Thailand, Hong Kong, Japan and back to San Francisco. Sally took me shopping in San Francisco for an appropriate wardrobe, as in Aspen there was no use for suits, ties, sport coats, etc., and I had long since spaced out my old college duds.

Thus outfitted, papered and transported, I headed off. The group I was traveling with included a husband/wife travel agent team, a couple of accountants, a retired couple, and two females roughly my age who worked as assistants in Congress. The presence of the Washington chicks was a constant source of worry, a perceived threat that was impossible to talk myself out of. They had to be DEA agents, narcs; they were on my trail and ready to bust my ass the minute any contraband came into my possession. And this was a three-week junket. God. The flight to Tokyo was incredibly long and tiring, and landing there and hitting the street was surreal. The sense of millions of people living in such close proximity, breathing the same polluted air, was palpable. It was such a close, stifling feeling, so hyper and smoggy, and it seemed like it was a national requirement to smoke cigarettes. We were booked into luxury hotels for the whole trip, the Hyatt Intercontinental in Tokyo, for example, so at least the accommodations were comfortable.

Each day there were planned excursions, a

real group tourism thing, and it became obvious early on that mine would be an acting job, 24 hours on stage (less sleep in single-room-time). "Oh yeah, I'm a ski instructor, teaching lots of folks, isn't is nice here in Kyoto, blah blah blah." Schmoozing with these straight people, the whole time with a growing sense of terror, dread, and apprehension about what was forthcoming. We cruised the Ginza and other sights, had deluxe dinners at the hotel. $50 for filet mignon, $100 for a good bottle of French wine. What would the old gang back home in the Valley think of this? From crowded, smoky, hyper Tokyo we went on to Indonesia. The first thing that happened upon our arrival at Jakarta airport was the checking of all health cards, which in my case revealed a lack of gamma globulin vaccine. Straight to one of the cramped side-rooms in the airport for a meeting with a morbid little military nurse and the largest, dullest hypodermic needle I had ever seen or had a nightmare about. It should be noted here that ever since I mutilated a couple fingers at age 16 and had to watch about twenty shots in my hand for local anesthetic, I was no great fan of shots of any kind. I don't know which veterinarian they had borrowed this implement from, but it could have been the one used on elephants, from the look of it. And talk about a civil servant who seemed to positively glow with pleasure in her work. This sucker felt like a sixteen-penny nail being driven, and hit me like an instant blast of the super-flu from a Stephen King novel. I don't know what effect one of these shots is supposed to have, or if the 95-degree heat was a factor, but I had to sit down for most of an hour to keep from hitting the deck. I felt like I had just come down with most of the exotic ailments known to man. My gut was churning, my head was spinning; I had shivers and a fever, and my skin was clammy as a damp towel. Welcome to southeast Asia.

They finally let me move and we caught our island hop to Bali. It was as if we had been transported back several thousand years; this was truly a mystical place. The people were smallish, moon-faced beautiful, usually smiling, with an aura of peace about them in spite if what seemed a poverty-level standard of living for most. The beaches were unspoiled, clean white sand, with spectacular sunrises and sunsets. There were shows at night at the hotel, with the Balinese dancers, all fluid and exotic eyes, the steel drum and strange instruments providing a soundtrack that was at once subtle and hypnotic.

One day I rented a motorcycle and hired a local guide, and we cruised all over the island, way into the interior, over narrow paths too tight for anything other than an animal or bike. One of our destinations was a monkey jungle, where you could buy bags of peanuts, then get swarmed over by literally dozens of monkeys, friendly but many large enough to inflict serious damage if provoked. The kind of miniature apes that looked strong enough to tear your arm off if they felt like it. They were regarded by the natives as almost deities, very respected, although when it was pointed out that Balinese sometime, ate a monkey's brains out while it was still alive on the table in front of guests, I wondered how much it really meant to be deified here.

At one point when we came out of the jungle into a clearing overlooking a river valley, the scene sucked my breath away. The valley was about a mile deep down to a winding stream, with the hillsides completely terraced and sculpted, many different hues of green, a valley that seemed to draw you down into it by just looking, a sculpture polished by many centuries of grooming. A vibration hung in the air that was at once serene and electric.

The most important destination for my guide was his village, where he wanted me to meet his parents. After another lengthy cruise through narrow, twisting jungle paths, we emerged into a clearing filled with about twenty grass huts with thatched roofs, built up on five- or six-foot platforms. Stopping at one, we were greeted by my guide's parents, and beckoned inside for the traditional coconut milk. His family was beaming as if I were some kind of dignitary. His father produced a large coconut, cut it, and we all shared the milk, which of course was quite delectable. The Balinese are all dark-haired and complexioned, but I had no idea how much of a novelty a tall blond-haired person was to them until we went back outside. It was as if the whole village had assembled, everyone smiling and friendly and reaching up to touch my hair. Their curiosity was genuine and benign, untouched by fear. Although somewhat embarrassed, I felt special in a way I never had before. A moment of purity isolated against the sordidness of my mission. From Bali it was on to Bangkok, the planned site of my surreptitious rendezvous with an unknown associate. We arrived in Thailand without incident, thank God, as my blood pressure was already on the rise just knowing where we were and why I was there. Promoting international trade. Talk about a humid sticky place with much squalor, fetid air, dirty urchins all over the street and everywhere fried bananas. It seemed like the poverty in the nation could have been caused by the historical squandering of wealth to build the massive solid gold statues that dotted the countryside. The value of a 50-foot-high, 24-carat solid gold Buddha seemed immeasurable — and ironic, when surrounded by starving children in rags. Maybe the poppy that was such an ingrained and revered part of Thai culture had served over time to dull conscience and common sense. The military presence was oppressive, yet the entire populace seemed stoned: glassy-eyed, stoical, zombie-like. My schedule called for me to be ill on a certain day and wait in my hotel room for a "visitor." Since we still had four-star accommodations, my only discomfort came from within. Sometime after lunch, Larry knocked on the door, gave me the code greeting and came in with his two bottles of Thai liquor, all sealed properly with the cellophane and stamps, a real professional piece of work. He said I'd never see him again; have a nice trip, see ya later, bye-bye.

And like that, I'd gone from smalltime to bigtime. I felt both exhilarated and stressed, my nerves on the verge of snapping. I had the bellhop send up a Thai girl for an hour or two of mindless fucking, the language barrier no impediment to the primal communication of dank flesh and come. At dinner I rejoined my fellow-tourists, and made bland excuses for my absence. "Yes, I feel okay now, must have been a bug, jet-lag or something. I'm fine now, thanks." It seemed we would never get out of Bangkok. My nervous system was in high gear. But leave we did, heading directly to Hong Kong.

What a charged-up place. At the disco on the top floor of our hotel I hooked up with some British and Aussie kids, and we partied all night, all over the city. I woke up the next day in some completely unfamiliar part of town, stumbled into a cab, and made it back to the hotel. I found everything in my room intact; I guess my "souvenir liquor" from Thailand looked too cheap for any self-respecting maid to bother stealing. We made it back to Tokyo for our last stop. I had a pleasant dinner with the more attractive of the Washington chicks, who professed a desire to take up skiing. Among other things. But if I no longer believed her to be a narc, I had developed another problem less than conducive to furthering our acquaintance. I was feeling an unpleasant sensation left behind by the lovely Thai girl, and I didn't think it would be a great idea to send something like this back to D.C., or anywhere else for that matter. I begged off and got to bed early that night, and alone. Another bad sign. The flight back from Tokyo to San Francisco seemed even longer than the first flight over, if that is possible. Adding to the discomfort, by now there was a strong burning sensation in my groin, and the carry bag with my liquors did nothing in the way of helping me to relax and enjoy the trip. I was sure there were spies on board, that I was already found out, just being given some leash before the big confrontation, the old shootout at the OK Corral. When you are so fatigued, bored, and jet-lagged and at the same time so paranoid, the mind can and does play many tricks, mostly not funny. By this point, on the last leg home, my social strategy was simply to play exhausted, too exhausted for any of the small talk and pleasantries that had been the staple for weeks. The moment was closing in on me with each passing mile. I was stirring in my seat, trying to sleep, read, watch the movie, anything to take my mind off that journey through customs. Then we finally were on the ground, deplaning, lining up, bumping, shuffling, heading for the fence. I remembered some of my training, or advice, and went for the line with the middle-aged female inspector, supposedly this was best. And I did my mightiest to appear sleepy, tired, and extremely bored. This was not an easy task, considering my situation. I had my bottles not hidden but in a small carry bag, right out front on the conveyor belt. She asked me the standard duty questions about what souvenirs I had, any produce or fruit, that sort of thing. After a cursory riff through my suitcases with not even a glance or mention of my liquor, and no duty charges to deal with, I was passed through and was out to the baggage area. Unbelievable! But the mind didn't stop there, as I was sure that I was still merely on that short lead and was being followed with the big swoop sure to come later, probably when I was making contact. Nothing to do now, however, but to play out the hand, so I retrieved the Caddy from parking, loaded up and drove downtown to the pre-arranged hotel and checked in.

As I got on the elevator to head up, I was followed on by two of the largest black men I had ever seen, both wearing nice suits. These dudes were over 6'6" and pushing 300 lbs. They regarded me silently. This I definitely did not need. I had thought the flight was long, but let me assure you that the 24-floor elevator ride was about a three-hour trip. I made it to my room where I placed my bottles in the bathtub, figuring that if the door got kicked in, I could at least have time to break two bottles, and lose all the evidence down the drain. I napped for a while, till the knock came at the door. Through the peephole I could see Jerry and at least he was alone. In line with all the other sleazy parts of the deal, he didn't have all the cash for me that we had agreed to. Had I been smarter (but obviously I still wasn't), I would not have turned over both bottles to him, but I just wanted done with this whole sickening episode right then. I was only too glad to see the end of the liquor and for that matter, Jerry. Now that I was clean, I spent about 28 hours tossing, turning, eating and sleeping. Once I came to what little was left of my senses, I couldn't wait to get out of that hotel. I had to go to a doctor's office for a massive shot of penicillin to take care of my ailment. Even a mundane little side mission like that went bad. As I was leaving the parking lot, a woman backed into the Caddy, damaging most of the passenger side. Just one more headache. I had to now go trade this beater in on another sled before I was finally on the road driving back to Colorado. I was at least so beat, so emotionally drained, that on this road trip I didn't see anyone following me the whole 18 hours. Imagine that.

Fall of '73 and back in town and back at work, I had still a strange feeling in my gut, kind of a foreboding, and the alien sounds and smells of Asia seemed to be in my senses all the time. It was as if I wasn't really awake, not really there. I still didn't dare to confide in anybody, couldn't talk at all about where I had been, just "Out in Marin County hanging with my girlfriend." It seemed like now I was just marking time, staying in place. The rest of my money that was to be forthcoming was of course repeatedly delayed, so I was on interminable hold. The Lode was rockin' as usual, and the girls were as much fun as ever, but I couldn't get those sounds out of my head. When there was not much of an early snow dump in Aspen, but reports of big storms north in Utah, the idea of a road trip sounded all too good, so a group of us got ready to go. Tommy Lee, a champion surfer, martial artist, and expert powder skier; Frank Woods, a prominent local real estate developer, though a beginning skier; Gerald, owner of the Lode and a classic powder skier, and myself.   We all piled with our gear into Tommy's crew cab pickup and off we went, to stay at Michael Lauer's (the coach's brother) house in Salt Lake City, our team headquarters. This was a real fun group of guys, and we made pretty good time, driving through storms all the way on Thanksgiving Day.   At Michael's place, we got all settled in on couches, spare beds, floors.   By the time we got up to Snowbird in the morning there was at least three feet of fresh snow and more coming down, about an inch an hour.

The skiing was incredible.   Gerald and I teamed up and we must have gotten 30,000 vertical by 2 o'clock in the afternoon. We were getting tired, but couldn't resist when we heard that the chutes in white pine were still untouched. These are out-of-bounds avalanche chutes and coloirs that you had to ride two lifts and then hike for a while to get to, but the reward was untracked, steep powder runs.   We were working our way from one to next, taking turns going first, each shot seeming better than the one before, just going crazy. I had pretty much put my previous activity out of my mind and was doing just fine, when we were hiking across a flat area en route to another chute. Suddenly, there was kind of a creaking sound and as I stopped moving, snow started to fall away out from under my skis. Not daring to move or even breathe, I waited until everything stopped moving and there I was, with like a hole under my skis. Looking down under the front of them, I could see down into some kind of mine shaft, deep, maybe 40 or 50 feet down, with the length of my skis spanning the abyss being the only thing keeping me from falling in. And from the depths was coming that weird Asian music and other sounds, moans and groans and desperate gasps. Death sounds. I gingerly sidestepped off the top of the hole, and tiptoed out of there as best I could in my Alpine ski gear.

A close call, another bad sign, a warning, unfortunately that went unheeded.

As we were coming up on the next chute, kind of idling across the flat, my skis hit something solid under the powder, some lumber perhaps. Going about 15-20 mph my skis stopped cold, throwing me on my face where I landed on a stump or log, a hard shot right to the solar plexus, right under my rib cage. I was hurting pretty badly, and knew that I was really injured when I felt like peeing, but was unable to. Gerald was worried but I told him to take off so at least one of us could put tracks in the chute, and I started the mile-long trek back to the ski area. This was a challenging, painful walk, to put it mildly. When I arrived at the top of the Gad 2 lift, all I could do was lie down on the floor of the little lift shack and tell the attendant there that I needed help. She called the ski patrol and one Eddie Licht showed up with a toboggan, gave me a cursory check and said "We've got to get moving right now." There was no safety chain on the sled so he just loaded me up, strapped me down and took off straight down the hill. At the bottom, they loaded me onto a stretcher in a van and hauled me up to the clinic. I was going down a different hill, and fast.

As I lay there in the clinic, I had flashes of Asia, and that music was getting louder in my head. I was becoming very sleepy. My vision seemed to be in a circle, gray on the outside, and the circle was becoming smaller by the second. My fingers and toes were balling up, and my pulse and blood pressure were flatlining. Then, in a flash, I could see my whole life, every second of my existence up to that point in perfect detail, things never remembered, being a baby in the crib, everything with amazing clarity all at the same time, all at once. And those sounds of southeast Asia, constantly echoing from some hollow chamber deep within my fading consciousness.Once they got an IV in my arm, and started to see a little bit of pulse blip on the screen, the doctors figured they could keep me alive for a while. And the small gray circle around my vision that had been becoming smaller and smaller began to stabilize and spread out again. My fingers and toes were uncurling and that fast movie of my life was gone; I was back in the clinic once more. I had been so tired, struggling to not fall asleep, as I was afraid I would not wake up. I was still exhausted, with a beat-up feeling throughout my whole body, but it was not quite so difficult to stay awake now. I was packed up, trundled into an ambulance, and rushed down to St. Mark's hospital in Salt Lake City. Once there, the ER doctors inserted a plug into my gut, filled me with about a quart of fluid, rolled me around some, and then drained me. The idea was to see if the plug came out full of blood, which would indicate internal bleeding, hence a ruptured spleen. They drained me and out came my blood, all of it. My spleen was completely destroyed. I was dry, running on fumes. Quick with the major anesthetic, and whisk me up to surgery, to remove the damaged goods, clamp off the arteries under the heart, fill'er up with some rapid transfusions and hope they wouldn't lose me somewhere along the way.

After fighting so hard and so long to hold on to that thread, I think my body, my whole being was still stuck in that mode. At one point I woke up in the middle of the surgery, surrounded by doctors, everyone a bloody mess, working in a buzz. Someone noticed and yelled, "He's awake, give him more gas!" They did and the next thing I knew I was looking at the walls and ceiling of a hospital room, looking from about three feet off the bed, floating in a morphine haze, knowing without a doubt that my condition had more to do with an evil than with skiing.

I was to be in that hospital for a week, at first in intensive care. I was supposed to have no visitors other than immediate family. But my ski pals of course were insistent on seeing me, and when Gerald with sandy hair, Frank with blond hair like mine, identified themselves as my brothers they were admitted readily. Then little Tommy Lee showed up, also as my brother. My boys, however, were nothing if not determined and we managed to have a pretty good little party, considering the circumstances. Since nobody else was at all aware of my recent travels, the whole incident seemed to them a Karmic joke without a punchline. But I knew different. We did come up with a new motto, though: "Don't sweat the NVO's" (Non-Vital Organs).

After a week in the hospital, I was released and flew back home to Fat City. It was now December 1973. There had been good snowfalls and everyone was skiing. This was entirely too frustrating for me, sitting around immobile, while all my buddies were cutting up the hill. What was I supposed to do, watch everyone else have fun, while I lay there like an old sick dog? Hell no. I dragged my sorry butt out to the airport and hopped down to Miami, to Mark's place so I could soak up some sunshine and heal my scars. This was a restorative week, sitting in the 80-degree sun every day with cocoa butter on my scar, Columbian gold in my lungs and the soothing salt air bringing me back around. After a week, I began doing some light workouts. Two weeks later I was ready to get back to the slopes.

And get back on the mountain I did, with a vengeance. Like I had always heard and accepted, when you are bucked off a horse, you must get right back on and ride, lest you be ruled and weakened by that fear forever. I started with three hour days of non-stops, and gradually increased until I was back to the all day hammer down non-stops that I had been used to. Since the doctors had told me that the only way I managed to survive my accident was by being in the peak condition I was in at the time, with survival fear as a motivator I was eager to get strong again. I knew that I had fucked up mightily by ignoring my gut and going along with the sleazy Jerry's plan. And when the mountains had punished my gut near immediately, somehow I knew that the mountains, the sport was true, if maybe unforgiving and harsh, still true and real. And while I went back to work at the restaurant and lived and partied much as before, I felt different. And though I could not then totally grasp what had happened, what I had done to myself on all levels, I think I knew, maybe not always consciously, but I knew in the winter of 1974 that life would never be quite the same.

Why should I not have to die

why should it be me

who gets to see

my own fast movie

and still be

around to be

all of the me

that I want to be

CHAPTER 9:

A Different Ranch, then Jumped Back to Music Business

For a couple of years starting in Winter 1974, I shared a house and lots of time with a very wealthy guy from Chicago named Joe Goldman. He was a very intelligent, screwed-up paranoid character, an extremely eccentric nutball with a crazy sense of humor, from an unusual background, to say the least. His family owned most of the movie theaters and drive-ins in Chicago, as well as TV stations, lots of downtown real estate, a movie production company in California, and God knows what else. This was all unknown to me when we met, then he was just another rich newcomer to Aspen who was friends with my friend Don Lemos, a local ski instructor and waiter, a very smooth guy who introduced us and said only that "Joe is all right". We ended up doing some horse trading with some different types of weed and maybe some flake and figured out that neither of us was a ripoff, and both liked to ride bicycles and ski (although he was even more of a beginner than me, not really very bold about it), and so we became friends. At some point our separate leases evaporated for one reason or another, and we talked about sharing a house. Joe couldn't buy anything in town, though he had the money, as this would change some tax position about residency or something his accountants told him, which meant nothing to me, so eventually he came up with a new, three-bedroom duplex on a lease in Mountain Valley, a newer subdivision on the east side of town, up towards Independence Pass. This was definitely upscale, streets carved out of an aspen grove up the hill, in the foothills really, with decks, and long views of the town and the east side of Aspen Mountain. And with Joe's truckloads of top quality furnishings, and million dollar art collection, we had quite a pad, Joe in the master upstairs, with me getting the two bedrooms and bath on the lower floor. It seemed pretty easy at the time, and turned out to be a great party house, earning the nickname "Gallery East" after a time, as our after-hours parties would sometimes be up to a hundred people getting absolutely trashed all night, going for greatness. It should be noted here that Joe was a gun nut and there were pieces of every type and caliber scattered all through the house, sometimes just laying on tables or standing in the corner, just part of the décor.

There were many funny incidents at the house, hell the whole setup was a cartoon. One time while we were out skiing, Pablo (my trusty Malamute) needed to get in, so he blasted through the screen into my room downstairs. Evidently this set off the alarm (Joe had the whole place wired with perimeter circuits, motion sensors, electric eyes, the whole deal) and the Sheriffs Department responded and went through the house to make sure there were no thieves there. When we got home from skiing, there was a note and a report on the kitchen counter. We thought it was amusing that no mention was made of the twenty or so guns laying around the house, or the pot plants on the porch, nor did it look like our little spice rack on the wall had been disturbed, after all it only contained weed of a couple varieties, hashish, and coke, in each of the little drawers. I guess mounted on the wall it really did look like part of the extensive art collection. Thank God for discretionary law enforcement at its finest!

At least some people knew who really paid their wages. Another time at one of our more splendid parties, an unknown guest was identified quietly to us as the newest undercover narc. Well, eventually he had to go outside to take a piss as the girls had both bathrooms tied up all night. That's when Snake Dog made his move. I'm not sure of course of any details, but word was the guy woke up the next morning on a bench or snow bank downtown. I guess he didn't get his chance to find out anything too much.

The parties we had were star-studded with celebrities, both local and international, our guest list would make the magazine rags envious, but to us it was just regular good time getting it on. Once when we came home from skiing, Joe's 911 Porche was sitting in our parking lot up on wood blocks, the wheels ripped off. After watching and listening to him rant and whine over his insured loss, I pointed out how fortunate he was to have been the target of a less than very intelligent crook who had gone through all the labor of jacking up the car and hauling off four wheels worth maybe two grand, when sitting right across the railing on the picnic table on the porch was a twenty-thousand-dollar Mark DiSuvero iron sculpture that maybe weighed fifteen pounds. This was funny, and eventually Joe stopped sniveling.

As I mentioned, Joe was very knowledgeable about art, classic, contemporary, sculpture, the works. Just being around all the books, pieces, and trading was an education in itself which I was grateful for, although like most good things, they come at some costs. In this instance the cost was lots of hours of brainstorming about what was to become his number one artistic endeavor, the Goldman Museum. You see, like many of us in that time, Joe became enamored with the Indian thing, Navajo jewelry, and later the weavings. Being quite intelligent and having an intellectual flair that I easily related to, we chewed and chewed and came up with the notion that to the first Americans, the weaving not of rugs but of wearing blankets was considered to be their highest, most valued art form. Indeed, in the 1800's one chief's blanket could be traded for several horses, many guns and a wife or two. So intellectually, we compared these pieces with the highest work of original European artists, such as Renoir, Dega, Picasso, etc. Therefore, Joe began collecting these artifacts, not for resale, but to place in a museum (with all the non-profit advantages) and went to Canoga Park, Ca., to Norman Rockwell's printer, a gentlemen in his late seventies, Guy McCoy, and commissioned the creation of poster size seriographs, twenty-some layered beautiful pictures. And he had a seal made with which each one would be stamped and numbered, a limited edition, much the same way as numbered prints of original paintings are made and marketed. The originals were on display in the

Goldman Museum, located on the top floor of Aspen's newest and most modern commercial building which also housed Abatone's fine restaurant in the basement, both of which were serviced by an elevator, a new concept in town at that time. We figured out how to hang the blankets on coat hangers padded by foam, and with the right combination of track lighting and spots, it appeared that the whole place was full of ghostly Indians. Combined with all manner of mind altering devices and a custom designed mega boom box sound system, there were many memorable hours and parties spent there. And as Joe liked to point out in private, he had devised a way in effect to legally print his own currency.

It was funny, but for a while after he started on the Indian trading business, he was just a mark for all the savvy Indian traders running around. And there were quite an assortment of these characters, from small players like Wolf, to major dealers like George Shaw, and Phil Holstein,

I mean major, guys rolling a couple hundred grand worth of tradables daily. At one point, Joe traded some bags of weed, some guns and a whole lot of cash for an artifact called the "den bundle". This was a dried buffalo scrotum filled with all manner of turquoise carvings (fetishes), necklaces, claws, bits of bones, feathers, and God knows what else. Well, he and a good friend of his from Beverly Hills, Steve Solo, our recent new roommate, jumped in the truck and headed down to Santa Fe to the Navajo nation headquarters as Joe figured he could trade this to the Indians for some really good pieces of weaving. As we know, things in those days didn't always come off according to plan. When they walked into the Navajo Museum and unveiled this bundle, all the women there covered their eyes and ran out of the room. Then, as the minutes passed with nothing much being decided, the parking lot and street out front begin filling up with Indians in pickups with full racks, just a whole bunch of them hanging around, not doing anything. Even though our boys were carrying pistols, as Joe explained later, even if they were able to shoot their way out of there, which was highly doubtful, how good would it really look for a couple of Jew-boys to shoot up the Indian museum and escape with Indian artifacts. So with a stroke of brilliant quick thinking on his feet, he announced that they had come there to make a gift to the Navajo Nation. Not being a person given to superstition or excessive religion, I nonetheless have to admit that this particular object was very strange, to put it mildly. When it was still at our house, one day I put on a turquoise jaw-claw necklace, at which point my dog Pablo started barking at me and wouldn't let me get anywhere near him. When I took it off and left it on the table he would come up all smiles and wagging tail and nuzzle me like always, but if I put it on again, he would go back to barking and whining and not come near me. Very strange, very strange indeed. And where before this little episode, the whole Indian thing was a major cash drain for Joe, after this every thing Indian he touched was a serious money maker. Go figure.

By now I had completely recovered from the loss of my spleen. I wasn't affected too much by not having the spleen, the only difference I could notice was not being able to recover from a serious drinking bout very well. I think that maybe it took longer for my blood to clean up, and if I got real drunk, I would have like alcohol poisoning for a couple days. The problem was that I was still haunted by the sounds and smells of Asia, and felt that the ski accident, and other bad things that happened were somehow tied up with guilt over what I had done. I was certain that this whole spleen thing was some kind of punishment for Asia. And I was coming to the realization now that I would never be fully compensated for my trouble, that the sleazy Jerry had probably never intended to pay what he owed. And since I had no leverage over him or means to force him to square up, this was just another loss to write off to experience.

Somewhere about this time in 1974, CC came in to the restaurant and told me that I had become a good skier pretty quickly, and she knew that I loved the sport and she wanted to hook me up with a young guy (who was briefly her boy toy, I think) named Tommy Simons, who was a local kid from the Aspen Ski team who had made the US Ski Team as a downhiller and who, she promised, could take my skiing to a new level. Since we had always been good friends I believed her and got together with T. So we met at his brother's ski shop one day and got ready to go up the mountain. Before we even got started, he looked at my boots, called me a turkey and said we would have to pretty much start from scratch. So I learned how to really buckle my boots, and we proceeded on up the mountain. He gave me a pair of 213 gs skis (he usually skied on 223 downhills) and started teaching me about going fast, real fast, and skiing like the racers ski. Before this I had an idea that I was a skier, but now I learned that I was a turkey, just thought I knew how to ski, and now I was learning. I chased T down the mountain for a whole season, skiing faster and faster, and we became best friends, running partners. Tommy then was a straight ahead super athlete, and a very generous, considerate person, who always went out of his way to help people, anyone anytime anyplace. The kind of guy who would pick up every hitchhiker and take them where they were going, even if it was out of his way. With shoulder length blond hair, he was definitely a hippie of the peace love variety, and had lots and lots of girlfriends, just a fun guy to hang around with. He got hooked up very early on with a group of weed smugglers, and did some trips south on sailboats, so always had large quantities of buds, and unfortunately, massive amounts of cocaine. In 1974, after we had trained pretty hard all winter, skiing top to bottom high-speed nonstops all day, he went to Italy and set the all-time speed record on skis at the KL (kilometro lanziato or flying kilometer) which was held each July at the Italian resort of Cervinia on the Italian side of the Matterhorn. This brought all sorts of fame and the coke craziness soon followed. Tommy became known as the Beast, as he would run for three or four days, 24 hours a day nonstop, then tuck in with one of the girlfriends and sleep for a day or day and a half, only to get up, shower, eat and start the party process all over again. After a while of this, things got a little ragged, and he became a little flaky, never where he said he would be, just on a roll, out of it, but still a nice guy, if you can imagine that. We would hang out at the ranch, playing darts, or horshoes in summer, and I even took him with me to Miami a couple of times. We always had fun and a lot of laughs, never hurt anyone but ourselves and just generally ran wild. But we did have our demons. When you snort that much, it is inevitable that the paranoia will pop up and we did our share of freaking and peaking, knew that we were being followed, that sort of thing. One time that Spring '75 we were going over to Crested Butte for a galendesprung (ski jumping) contest that had a Calcutta where we figured to make big bets and big money, as we figured T could out jump anybody. It was late at night when we set off on the six hour drive across the mountains, Tommy, Peggy (his current live-in) and myself in Tommy's four wheel drive Ford pickup. We were loaded for bear, carrying a couple ounces of blow, probably a quarter pound of Thai sticks, and several thousand dollars in cash for betting. We were barreling along about 80, with me driving, somewhere between Delta and Montrose, about 2 in the morning, nobody else on the road, when we came across a guy with a car parked, hitchhiking, trying to flag us down. This was at a turn in the road, which made the place totally secluded and the whole scene felt wrong to me, something was putting the hair on my neck up, I was feeling real edgy about the setup. I wasn't going to stop, but Tommy, ever the good Samaritan, would not hear of just driving past, said we had to stop. I was maybe fifty yards past the guy when I got stopped, and as I started to back up, I told T that I didn't like it, I smelled something funny. Here Peggy weighed in and said she too felt real bad about it, so as I was slowly backing up, I told T to keep his eyes on the guys hands. As we got closer, T leaned out the window and started calling to the guy "Hey, do you need some help?" We kept getting closer and T kept calling to the guy, who wasn't saying anything, not answering. He was walking towards the truck, and I could see that he had one of his hands stuck inside his jacket, which was zipped about half open. Tommy kept calling, we kept backing, though we were coasting with the clutch in and I had it in first gear, ready to launch out of there. This seemed to go on for a long time, though probably lasting only a couple of minutes. Time was stopped in freeze frame when we both saw the guy start to pull his hand out, even though he was only a few feet from the truck now and hadn't said anything in response to Tommy's questions. When he started to make his move, Tommy yelled "Go" just as I was dumping the clutch and burning out. We never saw if the guy had a gun that he was going for or not, but we were all real shaky for the rest of the drive. The next day we heard on the radio that there had been a shooting on that stretch of road the previous night, but never heard any details, even so, we knew from our instincts we had had a close call. After this, the contest was a washout, and while we didn't win thousands of bucks, we had a great party and felt lucky to be alive.

There were always more parties at the house, sometimes straighter dinner get togethers with non drug users, citizens, and some were the all-night type blowouts. At that time, we had taken in a third roommate, Steve, who was going with the actress Jill St. John, and she was one of the non-drug using type occasional guests, who was also into the better Indian weavings, and so was a customer of Joe's. Some days after skiing we would be invited to Jill's House in White Horse Springs, (near where Lori eventually built her castle) to hit the hot tub, which was always wonderful after a hard day on the mountain. And Jill was always gracious and fun to be around, not only beautiful, but a down to earth good person as well.

One day, Joe and Steve had arranged a sno cat tour on the back of the mountain with some of the movie crowd, Mort Heller, maybe Jill, and I don't remember who all else, about ten people altogether. These trips were a deluxe way to go powder skiing, as you would ride up the mountain in the sno-cat to virgin snow powder runs, ski down a couple thousand vertical, get back in the cat, ride up and do a different shot, all of it untracked powder. Steve was a pretty good skier, Joe was a promising beginner, and at this point after skiing with Abe for a couple of years, and with Tommy Simons, a lot, I was pretty much of a hot rod, which is why I was invited. What made the day become interesting was the little hits of acid we took at breakfast (the three of us), and mine must have been the strongest. Anyway, it was a perfect day, dark indigo blue sky, not a cloud and about two feet of untracked powder. When the vitamins kicked in I found myself unable to do three things. One, I couldn't cram in the snowcat with nine other people no matter how many movies they had done. Two, I couldn't make myself make a turn at all, it was too much fun to just stand on the 213's I was wearing and go straight down all the runs at about sixty (schussing). And three, I could no way wipe the ear to ear grin off my mug, so it was probably best that I was riding up on top of the cat with all the skis. What a fine day.

And missions, we went on lots of nefarious missions, in search of art objects, vehicles, ingestibles, ski highs, guns, and just about anything else you could imagine. One great car chase was really funny. We had heard about a mint original '38 Buick still owned by the old rancher who had bought it new and who was reportedly ready to let it go. So Joe and I packed up in his new Chevy one ton van along with Mary and Vickie, our girlfriends at the time, and headed down valley to Rifle to find and bring home the Buick. We took plenty of road weed, snorts, and a pile of Ben Franklins, along with a few guns to protect the girls, and were off in a fine humor. We get down there and find the car, but after much grinding on the old guy, he won't come down on his price, and Joe is sure this is too much to pay, or maybe just on principle he doesn't feel like giving any money to someone who won't knuckle under, I don't know. At any rate, we drove away without the Buick. We stopped for lunch at the only visible restaurant in Rifle, a little café that was all tile floor, standard truck stop tables and chairs, the obligatory hefty waitress, and a few good old boys in baseball caps and shitkicker boots camped out at the counter over their coffee cups. Real Americana. Anyway, we had some bad burgers or something, paid our bill and split, making it about twenty miles up the road with me driving when suddenly Joe started screaming, "Stop we've got to go back!" I'm doing about eighty, I don't feel like extending this fruitless mission any longer than necessary, so just keep the hammer down. Joe is real agitated though and keeps yelling "Stop, I left my vest at the restaurant." "So buy another one when we get back to town", I say, "They're only about twenty bucks, I'm in a hurry here". "No, he pleads, I left the cash in the down vest, and the blow"... I lock up the brakes, slide into a u-turn and start beating the pavement back to Rifle. This sounds like it could turn out to be a problem. As we come upon the restaurant there are no Sheriff cars in sight, but we are a little paranoid, so we break out the shotgun, and a couple of 44's (for what we really don't know), slide the van up near the door and Joe goes in. Well, big scare for nothing. In that simple, wonderful café, the waitress looked up as he came in, and just said, "your vest is on the coatrack by the door". Joe thanked her, grabbed the down vest, got in the van, and away we went. I still didn't register why all the fuss, until Joe took the 18 thousand in hundreds out of one pocket, and the three or four grams of coke and his driver's license out of the other. Oops.

We still had more and better parties going, sometimes with people like Steve Wynn from Vegas, John Denver, Spider Sabich, Mariel Hemingway, you know, what they call the "A" guest list. Some were decidedly less star studded, just your local funhogs and the illegal party favors. After one of these particularly boisterous gatherings, in fall 1975, our neighbors and landlord had had enough, bribes or not, so we had to move. A lady named Connie that I was hanging with at the time came up with a perfect solution, four acres out on the Old Snowmass Road behind the airport, with a duplex on it, a log-type structure with three bedrooms and three baths downstairs, and four bedrooms and three baths up. So I took out a lease option on the place, which also had a classic little red barn and three horseshoe pits, and subleased the upstairs apartment to David Rosen and his tribe, all from San Francisco and the summer ski camps in Chile. Joe had one master downstairs, and I had the other. The third bedroom we reserved for Miami Mark when he was in town. This little ranch was situated in a little valley with a steep hillside behind the house, and another across the driveway in front. Access was about a half-mile of curving potholed high-centered dirt drive that wound between a stand of Aspen trees. At the east end of the valley was a fairly prestigious subdivision named Buttermilk West, At the end of which ABC Dan had built his little chalet. This valley was known as Polecat Hollow, which became a case of the residents living up to their name.

We dubbed our little spread "The Ghetto Ranch" as in "The world is a ghetto". As part of our lease agreement we were assured by the owner, Andre Ulrich, owner of Andre's restaurant in town, that we were outside the city limits, and it was okay to shoot our guns any time we wanted. Music to the crazies' ears. Our downstairs living room was equipped with picture windows with the bookend smaller windows that would crank sideways completely open. We went out the hillside in front and wired a bunch of cookie sheets to the scrub at twenty and thirty yard intervals all up the hill and had a perfect target range with indoor shooting positions. We would get up in the morning, brew some espresso, have a doobie and maybe a line, crank open the windows, get comfy in the easy chairs with a windowsill rest and open fire with a variety of calibers. There is nothing like a fast 30 round clip from an AR 15 to get your juices flowing in the morning, and we were certainly not restricted by anything so silly as business hours, or nighttime, or daylight, or anything else. People used to ask us why we shot our guns so much and we would tell them, "because we ran out of cherry bombs". And imagine the social upper class guests arriving at the airport for their high-priced vacation in the toney little resort town, deplaning and while walking into the terminal being treated to the sound of automatic weapon fire. We couldn't understand how anyone couldn't appreciate the humor in the situation.

One of the best uses of peaceful weaponry came New Years Eve 1975, when one of the local coke whores showed up at the place in a taxicab with Gregg Allman and the chick from the movie "Nashville" in tow to try and score some coke from our tenants upstairs. They stopped in downstairs to appear to be socializing with us to disguise the real purpose of the visit, but of course we weren't fooled. And when Allman, who was obviously drunk or on downers and very obnoxious, started fucking around knocking over some fetishes that were part of Joe's little

Christmas display, and talking like he was a wannabe Negro, Joe started going nuts. And when they made their way upstairs for their true mission, he went for the M16. I said, "Come on Joe, I feel the same way but let's try to be a little creative here" "Okay Chuckles you've got about two minutes to get creative". After a couple minutes and me still stumped, he said "here, your turn" and tossed me the rifle. I opened the end window, stuck the muzzle out, and ripped off the whole 30-round clip. The roar inside the building was deafening, and closely followed by the clomp clomp of footsteps on the stairs as Allman and the girl fled to the cab, which took off at a high rate of speed down the driveway, accompanied by Joe's whistling a few 22 rounds thorough the trees as they went. I can't remember ever laughing much harder, and not feeling at all guilty, this guy was acting like a jerk, and he had just recently snitched off his longtime road manager, sending the poor guy to prison for 20 years. We definitely didn't need that type at the Ghetto Ranch.

One weekend when Aspen was hosting the annual Roch Cup, a downhill race on the prestigious World Cup circuit, Tommy showed up at the ranch with his best friend and mentor Steve McKinney. They had been on the US Ski Team together and Steve had won the Roch Cup downhill a few years previously, and was the first American to set the world speed record on skis. Steve was a big lanky guy from Lake Tahoe (Squaw Valley), a gentle longhaired hippie type, who was very intellectual and brutally honest. One of the most amazing skiers and mountaineers in the world, his feats were truly prodigious, yet he was an easy going fun loving guy, who nevertheless had an unmistakable intensity about him. We all became good friends and skiing with McKinney was a unique experience. He would cruise down anything at high speed, 70mph and up, without any movement except his feet, it looked like he was just standing still, though flying down the hill. And somehow he had misplaced his hiking boots the first day in town, so for a couple of days he either was skiing with ski boots on, or going barefoot, though this was in the dead of winter at 8000 feet. After skiing one day as we were standing around the bottom drinking beer I noticed Steve making little dams of the slush around the ski racks, (barefoot!) and when I asked him how he could do that he said

"It's all in the mind you know, I'm thinking of nice warm sand on the beach in Hawaii" Okay dude, I'd like to learn more about this kind of shit or something. Anyhow that was a good week in the little mining town.

Thing were cruising along at the ranch in fine style in 1976, skiing all winter, horseshoes, volleyball, tennis, and biking all the previous summer, with plenty of all-night dart games and parties to keep things balanced out. We had it all, literally the best of all worlds, both for substances and beautiful people. And all this so easy I guess is what began to be somewhat of a problem for me. I started to feel guilty, or if not exactly guilty, somehow remiss in not really making some contribution to the better good, or something like that.

Then one day I got a phone call from my brother in Ohio. Our father had had a heart attack and was in the hospital, not doing very well. I caught the first flight I could get and headed east. My father and I had always been very close, from when I was 4 and 5 and he worked nights, so spent lots of days with me, playing cribbage, canasta, pinochle, chess, just about every card game known to man. We had always gotten along well, even when I got freaky. He was a guy who said "If you can't say something good about somebody, don't say anything." A very considerate, gentle man who worked many hours in a tool and die shop so we kids could have extras, like piano and trumpet lessons, scouting, little league, just all good stuff. And he was always fun to hang out with, playing ping-pong, pool, swimming, fishing, just about everything. He always let me use his car for dates before I got my own, he even used to try to line me up with the cute girls in my class. He was from the generation that drank beer and whiskey and smoked Camels and worked hard. My buddies and I were always welcome to have one beer if we wanted, and all of us liked to hang out with him. When I got to the hospital and went into his room, I couldn't believe my eyes. He had lost massive weight, his face looked sunken, caved in and he could barely talk. I kind of went to pieces. I was not ready for this at this time. The doctors said that he could go home, but he would need professional care. Since he and my mother had divorced shortly after us kids had moved on, and my brother was busy in Cincinnati with his wife and five kids, the plan was for me to come back and take care of him in our old house which was empty. So I flew back to Aspen to try and put my life in order and move back to Ohio. This took a week or ten days to get organized, and then I got another call from my brother. He had died in the hospital. I flew back again to the funeral which was inadvertently scheduled on my 30th birthday, and I was a mess, racked with guilt about not getting back soon enough. I felt truly terrible now about all those years being gone and out of touch with my dad, after having been so close for my younger life. The sense of loss of him and of the time apart was difficult to bear. I had trouble getting over this, and it affected me I'm sure much more than I realized. After sorting out wills and assets and with a heavy heart I returned to Colorado.

And back home, back at the ranch, the tragedies just kept on coming. David, my upstairs tenant, was a strange, reclusive little fellow. Although very bright, and from a very wealthy family, he had a serious cocaine habit. He would be in pajamas and bathrobe for weeks at a time, walking around the house with a little bowl full of snort and a Bic pen barrel for a straw. Just like a friendly zombie, spaced out, wired, talking gibberish, unbathed, unkempt, a real mess. And from Chile or wherever, there seemed to be an endless supply, I thought he probably had a couple kilos buried out in the barn or something. Harmless person, but a real mess. Then one day, for some reason, he had gotten cleaned up and dressed and went into town over to Tommy's house at Fourth and Smuggler which was a hangout, party house and where a little group always went to watch Star Trek at 4 o'clock after skiing. I was on my way there after skiing when I ran into one of the girls walking about a block from the house. "Don't go over to Tommy's, she said, there are ambulances and cops all over the place, something real bad is going on." Real bad is right. David was dead, and the story was very unusual, to say the least. It seems that while smoking a roach using a hemostat as a roach clip, he had had an epileptic seizure, and in the midst of his thrashing about, had managed to jam the hemostat into his ear, killing him. I don't think any of us even knew that he was an epileptic. Whew! This was in late February 1976, and after coming back from my sad time in Ohio, was more than unsettling, was real freaky. This was too bizarre to comprehend, wasn't something I could even think about, just a mind-blower, a numb shock, there aren't even words that fit. I was antsy I needed a change, it was time to make a move.

One good thing that happened was that I had gotten together with a beautiful lady named Alan. She had long thick black hair, deep hypnotic eyes, and just as important, a tranquility about her that made me feel calm and solid when we were together. She felt as soothing as cool lotion on a blistering sunburn. She was bright, educated and articulate, with a wonderful sense of humor that enabled her to smile about most of life's absurdities. A very grounded, stable woman. I was protective of her, always keeping the business and any large amount of product far from her. She knew about the weed, but didn't judge me; in those days, being a mover still accorded a kind of celebrity status. To say I was smitten would be an understatement: I had found my soulmate, my true love. Everything about my life seemed better with her part of it.

Back in the Basalt days, Michael, the guitar player from my band who had gone to LA where he had put together another group, got signed to a major management company (Mace Nuefeld), recorded an album, and almost made it happen. Key word here: almost. Now in 1976, after this had all come apart, he was in Hawaii and kind of regrouping on the beach and teaching guitar through one of the larger music stores there. Now we got back in contact with each other and started talking about putting another project together. This felt like what I needed to do at the time, sort of a scratch for my artistic itch. Along with my friend/girlfriend Connie from Chicago, we made a loose agreement with Joe that we would do the initial startup, get Michael back to the mainland with some backup musicians, then Joe could bring in his big contacts and/or bankroll the deal.

So off I went to Hawaii to talk Michael into giving it another shot, and soon he was at the ranch, and we were pulling players in from all over the country, rehearsing, building what in our minds would be a supergroup. A good concept, but of course one shown by hindsight to have flaws. One being that for whatever reasons, after Connie had rounded up a few thousand dollars from some of her friends to launch the thing, Joe refused to come through with anything, causing much animosity with Connie, and me caught in the middle, possessing only a fraction of the required resources, not to mention diplomacy. Tommy was real impressed by the music and hooked us up with some of the Colorado boys he had been working with, and they ponied up some cash to help out and between Connie and I we squeezed as much out of the Chicago action as we possible could and we were giving it a shot. Part of the package had me not doing any more dealing now, so as to keep the project clean and not unfairly risk the freedom of a bunch of innocent musicians. But with Joe, there were now too many strong bad vibes, there were too many people and too much energy involved to drop the project, so I had to invite him to leave so we could use the entire house and energy to forward the cause. This was a no win situation, and I felt bad about this, and I'm sure Joe must not look too kindly on me for it either. And when we started to lose momentum here in Aspen, we changed our headquarters to a large house in Bel-Air (LA) that I leased over the phone. This made sense because we would be in the heart of the music business, and in close proximity to our good friend, Terry Kath, guitarist for Chicago, who had always been impressed with Michael, and had agreed to get us a label deal with his manager and label.

So now in 1976, I had been a card carrying local for years, probably some kind of fixture on the social scene, (I won't even attempt to say what kind of fixture), had become if not one of the most elegant, surely one of the fastest and strongest skiers on Aspen Mountain, now here I was leaving my beloved valley. I had taken some hard hits, lost my father, almost lost my own life, and was still kind of under a funky gloom of guilt over betraying my gut with the Asian thing. You could say that I had lots of mixed feelings about making this move, but overall I felt that maybe I could be doing something more artful, more productive on a higher plane than all the hedonistic partying in town. That somehow I needed to make up for something, to do something. Like I say, my feelings were kind of mixed up, scrambled, and maybe I was just trying to run away from something as much as running into something. At any rate, I told myself that this was just a mission, I wasn't really moving out of Aspen, I was still a local and always would be. For all the questionable crazies there, there was a very solid core of locals, some of the finest people to be found anywhere that I was still fortunate enough to be able to count as my friends.

We were working hard rehearsing and writing material, assembling a group of excellent players, already in the studio making demos when Terry was killed in a tragic incident at his house with a Luger. This horrible accident proved to be a crusher for us, we were out of funds, in hock to the Chicago boys and some of the Colorado guys, and now with no record deal. This spelled the end of the noble experiment, and I was trying to figure out what to do about a house I couldn't afford to pay rent on, a bunch of musical equipment I couldn't pay for, and just generally how to eat, as I had tossed everything I had into the kitty. Then the phone rings, and its one of my old ski buddies, Marty, who has been working in Miami, he's right in town and happens to have a few bales of primo Columbo, and did I know where to help him unload some? So even though I had thought I could forego the business and return to a higher calling, my back was to the wall, or I was weak, or whatever you want to call it, but yes, I did know some people in LA and I could help, and just like that I was rolling again, seemed like I could never stop.

you say this is it
what a good fit
don't take any shit
everybody's doing shit
take another hit
just a little bit
you think you're the shit
then you just feel like it
now you know its time to git

CHAPTER 10:

Too Fast, Too Cocky, and the Walls Cave in

The Beverly Hills scene was pretty crazy too, like everything else those days of 1977. My friends there were from wealthy families and had big mansions. Most of the parents were divorced and/or gone and the kids had the run of the estates. We would be shuffling bales in and out in the middle of the day, with never a worry or a problem. For sport we used to go to the local Budget car rental and rent new luxury cars on the weekend or weekly special, then run them through their local thrashing course and just brutalize them, laughing uncontrollably the whole time. We had a course that would begin at Sunset Boulevard and head up Benedict Canyon; at Tower Road there was a drain bump, and if we had the accelerator floor-boarded from Sunset and steered way over to the right next to the curb to hit the drain bump, we could launch and get major air time. Yahoo! Then we would proceed up the canyon to a little dirt road, turn off, which was a couple miles of winding dirt road through the back country, past and through some fine hidden estates round several big high speed curves and switchbacks and eventually dumping out on Beverly Glen, which would wind like a smooth GT course back to Sunset. This was the local kids' shakedown course and it was a killer one indeed.

One day we had rented a brand new Mercedes-Benz 450SEL with about 200 miles on the odometer. Well, of course, we had to put it through the test. We got it up to about 80 and by Tower got massive air time, but being so heavy the Benz bottomed out in the front on landing with a bang. By the time we finished the course and pulled into Sandy's driveway and shut down, the car was spewing oil all over the driveway, running into the sidewalk and yard. Uh-oh, bad boys. What do we do now? We came up with a brilliant plan. We called Budget, irate, raising all kinds of hell about how their German piece of shit was leaking oil all over the property, the gardener was going to have a fit, what was wrong with you people, etc.. It worked. They were very apologetic and dispatched a tow truck, clean-up crew and another 450, which they gave us for the week, no charge. It's amazing what you can achieve with a little attitude and a lot of bullshit.

So things started to move again and we were working LA pretty regular, using Sandy's Beverly Hills house for work and parties, bouncing back and forth back to Aspen.

Parties with lots of hookers, one of whom seemed to be Sandy's semi-permanent roommate. But although business (just weed) seemed to have great promise, something was beginning to feel off, not right. A harder edge seemed to be taking over the action.

Alan had a month-long trip to Europe planned with her father. While she was gone, I had a couple of short hops to LA to keep myself busy. But I was excited when the day came in Aspen that I heard she was back. I prepared to meet her at the Mother Lode for dinner that night at 7:30.

But when eight rolled around and she had yet to show, I began to worry. She was one of those people who was prompt to the point of being early before she'd be five minutes late. I drove over to her house to find ambulances and police cars all over the place. The scene seemed more surreal to me than the most bizarre drug-tableau of Southeast Asia. I knew what was coming, and yet I didn't. Something bad, something worse than my imagination wanted to register.

And it was. An improperly installed wire in the shower had come in contact with the metal stall, and Alan, spritzing off in anticipation of our date, had been electrocuted in her own bathroom.

Added to my other losses I think that for a few months I was in some kind of grief-numbed, drug-numbed cloud. The senselessness of her death bled into all other aspects of my life, making them too seem utterly without pattern or reason. Some truly rotten people were starting to appear in the drug world, hard and "professional." As a result, there was a certain amount of apprehension on all ends that was new, and unwelcome. And then good old Spider, Spider Sabich, the ski champion, golden boy, star, media darling and all-around fun guy. A good-timer. Spider was liked by everyone. He was really a nice guy, not stuck on himself, just one of the boys. Like most of us, he would do any chick he could as long as she was cute, whether it was his old lady, yours or mine. I think that this American "rock 'n' roll" permissiveness was a little too foreign for the French Claudine, who was very much the jealous type. One day, shortly before the fateful Sunday, she had apparently seen or heard of Spider hanging out with some other woman. Lee, the bartender told me she launched a pitcher at him in Cooper St. Pier, narrowly missing his head, the pitcher shattering against the stone support pillar next to him.

Not long afterwards, a group of us, Spider included, were drinking beer again in Cooper St. Pier after skiing. We were making plans to fly out to the Vegas ski show the next day. What happened when Spider got home to Claudine is history, very sad. Claudine was and probably still is a lovely person, though with a temper. Whether or not drugs were involved no one knows, but the blow can certainly lend a certain edge to an already volatile personality at times. Not everyone in Aspen agrees with me, but I believe it was just a very unfortunate accident. He was showing her how to use the gun; it went off in her hand; Spider bled to death from a bullet through his abdomen on the way to the hospital. But undoubtedly some of Spider's other friends thought there was a lot more to it, and they were very vocal in the bar about being bitter about Claudine's "slap-on-the-wrist," 30-day jail sentence for criminally negligent homicide. Claudine ended up marrying one of her defense lawyers, which didn't exactly serve to change some people's minds about her "innocence." But regardless of what may or may not have actually happened, Spider's death and Claudine's trial put Aspen on the map for the tabloid set.

All this bad feeling still did not totally dampen my attraction to the action. I had a big bad Benz, pocket full of cash, good looking women, constant buzz on, and thought I was the shit. Just a little too full of myself for sure, but what did I know. One day in L.A., kind of out of the blue, I get a call from Tommy, who is right down the street with Steve Mckinney, in a broken down van wanting to know if I can pick them up and help. Of course I can and after we get back up to the house they tell me what is going on, which is that they have come back from Italy with a load of ski gear from one of the Italian manufacturers that have sponsored them and need help starting a company to market this brand in the US, as they have exclusive rights. There followed a series of phone calls, interpreters, faxes and general activity to try and come up with a plan. I had no experience or know-how particularly in this field, nor did they, but we naively assumed that our good intentions and enthusiasm would carry us through. It was finally decided that Steve, a lawyer friend of his from Reno, and I would fly to Milan to sign contracts, so we would have something to build on. Steve went over early to take care of some other business, and the lawyer and I would travel together and meet Steve there. This trip was an interesting adventure from start to finish, as I was to learn was true with all things involving McKinney. When I went to the bank with my girlfriend Sally in San Francisco I bought $1500 worth of travelers checks, put them in my briefcase and left. Only when I was on the first leg with the lawyer SF-NY and I was going through my papers did I notice that the bank had given me $2500 of checks. The lawyer assured me that I had done nothing wrong and the best course of action was to merely spend the money, not to worry about any ramification, just feel fortunate. Okay. Now just before I left LA I had scored a couple ounces of killer Hawaiian buds, which I had packed into one of my cowboy boots in my suitcase.

After we deplaned in Milan and moved to the luggage area to collect our bags and clear customs, we spotted Steve, right on schedule, with one Quinto Lazzaroto, an 85 year old Italian gentleman and FIS official and good friend of Steve's, who was to be our liaison for our dealings in Italy. We waved to them on the other side of the fence, and began looking for our luggage. I saw my big Lark bag coming down a long conveyor belt with all the other bags heading our way. But then to my horror, I spotted a soldier with a German Shepard on a leash walking on top of the conveyor belt and bags from the other end heading towards mine. I was starting to freak, then just went for a fast move, said "There's my bag," jumped up and grabbed it and headed for the check-in. I didn't know what kind of nose the dog had, but sure didn't want to gamble on it one way or another. And to my great pleasure and surprise, no one challenged me or even seemed to notice and like that I was through customs, on the other side of the fence, shaking hands with Quinto and Steve, throwing everything into a ski company Opel station wagon that Quinto had brought, and off we went. No problem, and like that we were in the wagon whizzing down the Autostrada at 160km (100mph) while Quinto, with one hand on the wheel busily pointed out the sights and keeping up a steady travelogue in his thick combination of Italian and English. Not to worry. After a couple days of contract negotiations with several companies, the lawyer took the papers and flew back to the States to begin structuring that side of things, leaving Steve and me free to do some publicity tours (Steve was very much a celebrity in ski conscious Europe, along with Tommy known as the "flying hippies"). First, though we had checked into the Jolly Hotel to recover form our jet lag and pretty much laid up and smoked the good weed and ordered room service about four or five times a day. When we finally went out and got to the lobby, all the hotel help were smiling at us which we could not understand. Only when we went back up to our suite, which was right across from the elevator, got out of the elevator did we comprehended the smiles. The whole floor reeked of Hawaiian. We were cracking up too much to be worried, besides if anyone was going to do anything, we figured it would have already happened by now. Steve got on the phone and found an Italian friend of his, Paolo, who came by and socialized with us for awhile, then we made plans for Paolo to pick us up in the morning and go up to Cervinia to ski. Before Paolo arrived in the morning, though, Steve had been on the phone to someone in Chile, and somehow decided that he had to head there immediately. So like that Steve was heading to the airport, having left me his skis to use and a friends hotel in Chamonix, France to go see next, have fun, Ciao for now, see you later. Then here comes Paolo and off we go to the Matterhorn. Talk about a fast mover as well as fast skier.

Actually, the promo trips with Quinto are worth mentioning, as we were being liasoned by one of 12 Italians out of 1000 to have survived a WWII Nazi death march back to Italy, a short fireplug shaped man of incredible energy and good spirit, a prototype butt-pinching dirty old man going after all women, just an amazing character. At any meal when one of us would order mineral water to drink, Quinto would ask us if we wanted to die tomorrow, change the order to wine and proceed. And when we would stagger to our rooms at night, drunk and wobbly, while Quinto was still in the bar drinking and carrying on, we would never imagine that we would have the little sucker banging on our doors at about 7 o'clock in the morning, showered, shaved, dressed, and ready to go skiing. What a guy.

One of the pr stops was at the resort of Marileva, where in addition to the hours of photo shoots where Steve would graciously pose with moms, kids, everyone it seemed, they had set up a mini speed course, so they could photograph Steve flying by in his tuck. The problem was, not being racers, they didn't realize that he would hit the photo area going about 80 mph and no way could stop in the little space they had set up there. So here comes Steve for the cameras, jumps a bench and goes tearing down the access road heading down the mountain. About an hour or more later he finally makes it back to the resort after barrelling down this narrow switchback road, too narrow to turn or stop, for about five miles, then having to ride a couple of trams and lifts to rejoin the party. Steve said this was one of the hairiest runs he had ever taken, during what was supposed to be a picnic. Of course being the type of person he was, he was full of good humor about the whole thing, just cracking up.

Then, since Quinto had been called to Rome for something the day before, we had to get up at 3am to catch a bus ride down the mountain, through lots of little villages to get back to Milano. We were the only people on the bus at that hour, so loaded our gear, skis and ourselves on the two back rows of seats, and promptly crashed out for the ride. At some point we were awakened with radios blaring and a full busload of people crawling all over us pointing and laughing. It was real funny, so with broken Italian we joked with the folks all the way back to Milano.

After some memorable ski days on the glacier at Cervinia skiing with Paolo, and clubbing at night with him and his Sicilian pals, I got on the train and headed to France. From Paolo I had gotten a big golfball sized chunk of black Afghani hashish, which he showed me how to melt, then mix with tobacco and roll into a joint, rolling up a little piece of cardboard form a matchbook to make a filter. I had just smoked one of these when some uniformed guards came into my compartment and started questioning me in

French, which I spoke not a word of. I was confused and on the edge of panic when I finally figured out that they just wanted to see my papers and evidently hadn't noticed the aroma in the compartment. (I had the window down, but what did that mean?). We had just crossed a border and after checking and stamping my passport they were on their way. Of course once my adrenalin stopped pumping I rolled another one and had a nice ride into Chamonix. I took a taxi to the Hotel Sappiniere and as I went trudging up to the entrance lugging my two suitcases, briefcase and 215 cm skis, a fellow came out of the hotel to greet me and said "we saw your big skis and figured you were a friend of McKinney's" I confirmed the fact and was led to a delightful third floor corner suite that I was told was where Steve and Tommy always stayed when they were there. It seems that the hotel was the second oldest in Chamonix, a beautiful classic ski town in the French Alps, having been founded by Patrick's grandfather. Patrick now operated the place, with the assistance of his American born wife, and I spent a good time there skiing Mont Blanc and dining royally at the hotel, then sharing a smoke at the desk with Patrick and his associate Alain.

All too son I was low on funds and it was time to train to Geneva, then fly to New York's Kennedy airport where I had another small luggage fiasco. I had been given lots of samples, ski pants, sweaters, boots, etc. by the manufacturers, and while in Milano I had bought at great savings some cashmere sweaters, shoes, suits, silk ties, and before landing had properly filled out my duty declarations and was prepared to pay several hundred dollars in duties. I also still had this big ball of hash and decided to just keep it in my hand and if it looked like I was about to be rousted I would throw it on the floor into a crowd. Good safe strategy, a well thought out plan, yessiree Bill. The problem was that when I went to the baggage area, I couldn't find my suitcases. They were nowhere to be found. As I went through the customs line and told the officer I couldn't find my bags, he laughed and said they would probably show up the next day in Brazil or someplace. I didn't really see the humor in this, but with the big ball of hashish in my mitt I wasn't about to start something with him. So he signed off on my duty slip but before leaving I cruised the whole area again, and there in a corner Lo and behold my missing luggage. With my duty card already signed off, I just picked up my stuff, went through, turned in my card, and went to the domestic section for my flight to Denver.

I had decided to cruise through Aspen for some skiing on my way back to LA, and after traveling for weeks, flying all night, got a connecting flight into Aspen at about 10 am, totally jet lagged whacked out, got picked up at the airport by Abe, who took us straight to the mountain, insisting we go skiing right now. What a pal. That day was very high speed, a total blur, complete with joints and naps on the lifts (ever try sleeping on a chair lift?) and beers and blow after skiing, followed by 24 hours of sleep. Fun fun fun. The next stop of the magical mystery tour was Vegas, for what reason escapes me, but there I was at McCarren airport with my ticket to LA and about $28 cash and no more. I had sold the Benz before I left, taken a deposit, and was supposed to pick up the rest of the cash upon my return. The problem was, I had been unable to reach Jerry, the guy who had the car, and I could only keep leaving messages. Before I got on the plane, I bought $20 worth of silver dollars, gave one to the change girl, smiled and asked which slot we could make some dough on. Without hesitating, she pointed at one and said, "Play that one". Of course I did, hit a $300 jackpot, gave her $40, got on the plane, landed in LA, checked into the Ramada Airport hotel, left Jerry a message, had dinner and went to sleep. The next morning, like clockwork Jerry called, picked me up, paid off the car, and I was on my merry little way again. Nothing like an average normal road trip. The good luck and good spirit of this trip told me that I wanted out of the drug trafficking thing, which I'd been doing since Marty's call, that I wanted to associate with the clean energy of McKinney and his business projects. For while he liked to get high some and party some, he would never do anything criminal, dealing or the like. He was just such a clean honest spirit, that I wanted to change from what I was uncomfortable becoming. So I told myself that I would just put together this one last good project, take the money and run. Unbeknown to me, an age old sad story.

Whether it was my own damaged psyche or the changing nature of the trade itself, things were feeling a little off – strange, tough, paranoid. These were pretty much the unsettling feelings that had begun after Asia, which not only hadn't improved, but if anything, had gotten worse even now in 1978. It seemed like every day and night something would resonate, or trigger, and the sounds and smells would be back, and I would be kind of off balance, not quite sure where I really was, and timings would get ragged, being just too early, or just a fraction too late. I kept going anyway, what could I do? I had a meeting with the Maleno brothers, from the old Little Annie gang, who had kept expanding and expanding and were now loading and sending boatloads of Columbian. I would, along with Sandy, lease a secure "load house" in a secluded setting, with a large lot with a garage so that we could warehouse most of their load, for ten dollars per pound, and then have access to as much as three thousand pounds to move ourselves, which we could make as much as 50 dollars per pound on. After all the dust settled, we should end up with around 100,000 dollars each, and I would be gone, checked out of the scene, stopped finally. I got ahold of all my movers and told them to get their people and cash ready and we found a big house in the valley at the top of a hill up a long driveway, tucked into the trees with a pool and big garage, just perfect. We got all settled in and set up and pretty soon here came the boys in a big flatbed truck with a container on board, right around a ton of bales. These we broke down and dispersed among our local movers over the next couple of weeks. Then came time for the second shipment, and this was when the shit hit the fan.

The brothers were supposed to have made advance arrangements with me, but when I got back from running errands one day, Sandy informed me that the boys were on their way and due any minute. I started to get a creepy sick feeling in my stomach. We weren't ready; the garage was still "dirty" from the first load, empty containers and about 600 pounds still there. I raced around cleaning up as best I could, throwing everything into the shell of my Nissan truck.

Then the boys were there, backing the big rig up to our garage door. But there was a hole in the plywood container, which was stamped "machine parts," and it struck me as ominous. Giving in to pure instinct, I jumped in my little truck. I had to get out of there, and fast.

I was across the lot barely on the driveway when out of nowhere a helicopter came whipping over the ridge of trees and was hovering right above my hood. Three cars had ripped up the driveway, and in no time two big guys wielding 9-

milimeters were in my face, dragging me out of the cab. We were nailed with over a ton of weed.

The narcs carted everyone else away, but cuffed me to the sofa inside while they hung out for a couple hours, answering the phone and trying to suck other people into the sting. Right under the sofa to which I was chained was my automatic 12-gauge Remington, completely illegal and loaded to the max. My paranoia swelled. I was being set up to be "justifiably" killed; the cops would find the weapon and blow me away in "self-defense." I never thought being carted out of my living room in cuffs could feel like such a relief, but when the alternative (in my mind, at least) was being wheeled out on a slab, the slammer seemed like El Dorado.

We were to remain in LA County Jail for several days, until the family got bail reduced from $500,000 to $50,000 and everyone taken in the sting was released. A couple weeks later I was offered a "deal" – not by the Feds, but by the family: plead guilty, take the fall, and get a $100,000 compensation upon my eventual release from prison. It dawned on me then that the brothers must have struck a deal even before the first load arrived, and the second delivery had just been Playhouse 90 with the DEA in hopes of entrapping more people. This was how far the idealistic 60s-good-guy hippies had sunk. One of my attorneys educated me as to how the game was played. He told me about "three-fers," getting those apprehended to set up three others in exchange for their freedom. This was now standard operating procedure for the police. Some of the biggest dealers had turned government agents. So much for our old outlaw code and hippie self-righteousness. It was just a mean scene, double-dealing, selling out, all the same.

The heroes, if there had ever been any, were either dead or sold out. No more honor among thieves, but only greed and deception. The whole world had gone crazy upside-down; the 60s were long gone and with them any vestige of innocence and Robin-Hood idealism. Bad dreams, sleepless nights, and the nightmarish sounds that now mingled the whirr of police helicopters with the surreal music of Southeast Asia.

Just a few weeks earlier, I had thought that I had it all together. I had had lots of girlfriends, waitresses, stewardesses, actresses, famous daughters, heiresses. I thought I was quite the stud, but I was really hopeless, as I loved them all.   Money to burn, lots of good bud and blow, the fat pad, skiing, tennis, generally a pretty easy lifestyle.   So I thought.   But now it was all in tatters.   Everything was gone, even many friends and loved ones.   My world was shattered and my mind was reeling.   It was the end of a decade and so much more.   I didn't have much idea where to turn, what to do now.   All I knew was that I could not stop, I had to get back home, back to my mountain, back to Aspen, which is where I headed.

I didn't take the "deal", instead went through a lengthy boring trial only to be convicted and sentenced to three years in prison.   I immediately had my lawyers file for an appeal, so since I had posed no problem for the last few months out on bail, this was continued.   And since I was from Colorado and had promise of a job and housing, I was allowed to transfer my probation supervision and move back there, though with no idea how long the appeal process would take, much less what the outcome would be.   Now I had not only the haunting sights and sounds from Asia with me, but also some new bad helicopter movies in my head to go along with the many-layered pleasures of my new in-limbo state.

And did you really think
that nobody would blink
that you could sink
down to the brink
and be the link
to the terrible stink
that makes their blood run pink
and heads all out of sync
that you would just give a wink
and away you could slink

IN TRIBUTE TO:

Meta Burden

Wife of Doug Burden (very nice people from back east possibly Vermont), excellent powder skier, killed in avalanche in Walch's Gulch, out-of-bounds territory off the east side of Aspen Mtn. towards Independence Pass. Meta was pushing the envelope, skiing back country alone on a day of questionable snow conditions, and paid with her life. She was much loved and missed by all who knew her.

Fritz Stammberger

Fritz was Austrian, a big strong world-class skier and mountain climber. He would ski many days on Aspen Mtn. without gloves to train and condition his hands for assaults on K2, Everest, major expeditions. He had a great sense of humor, a fun-loving guy in a serious business. He would come into the Lode, slam two Heinekens and leave as a normal routine. Not one, not three, just two. Fritz went missing in Afghanistan.

Lance Reventlow

Barbara Hutton's son, developer and campaigner of the Scarab road racing car, and avid skier and generally pleasant person. Lance died in a plane crash with four other Aspenites, a single engine Cessna that went down up Independence Pass, all wealthy individuals, the grim reaper makes no exceptions based on net worth.

Michael Pokress

Michael was a long-time waiter at Andre's restaurant and strong, expert skier. A stocky muscular guy, nevertheless very gentle with an unassuming kindly manner, very well-liked. Michael became a real estate agent, was very successful in a short time, and was in a small plane with some clients heading across pearl pass en route to Crested Butte, when their plane collided with another one heading from Crested Butte to Aspen. Michael and all others perished.

Doug Pimental

Former Aspen resident who had moved to Crested Butte and had a ski shop there, was on the plane that collided with Pokress'. Everyone on this craft died instantly also.

Charlie Starr

Local freelance mechanic, hustler, etc. Heavy set, somewhat sloppy appearing person, a little rough around the edges, but a good-hearted although somewhat loud, brash character. Part of the Pub crowd, an accomplished beer drinker. Died from an ingested chemical imbalance.

Pat Baz

One of the long-time local good guys. Waiter and partner at Pinocchio's Parlor for years, later one of the original crew at Galena St. East Steak House and top waiter there for years. Lived at Carter's house with the volleyball court with cute Tawni from Chicago. Died from an ingested chemical imbalance. Missed by the whole community.

Ron "Gloves"

Salt of the earth hardworking mechanic, generous without bounds, longtime employee of the old Martin Bishop at Bishop's garage, slight back east transplant, drove a battered 1948 Lincoln Continental convertible. Accomplished Pub sitter and beer drinker, pal of Nutty Ned. Put his 9 mm in his mouth and ended it all. Not an enemy in the world. Missed.

Vladimir "Spider" Sabich

Ski racer star, everyone's golden boy. Hot Rod party animal, loved by all, much charisma, a fun person to be around. Tragic accident with longtime girlfriend Claudine Longet and a handgun. Much loved and missed.

"Honest John" Tange

Tall, lanky guy with a wandering and a quiet gaze who could be quite unsettling. Very nice person, who enjoyed fighting and brawling more than anything. Would always back up his word, a person to be counted on. Bought a ranch back home in Montana with wife Harriet. Died in a Harley crash in Sturgis. Well-liked and respected by all who knew him.

Thomas "Mack" MacCauley

Red-bearded Irishman from Chicago, a hardworking highly skilled stone mason who did much of the spectacular rock work on the high-dollar Aspen homes and buildings. Mack was one of the town patriarchs, revered and respected by all, the guiding influence of what was right and proper in our new-age, evolving little society. He always spoke from the heart and backed it up with actions, regardless of the cost. Our grandpa, our Pope, stern but fair, overstuffed with kindness and good cheer. Ran his Triumph motorcycle off the road racing down Independence Pass and was killed. Loved and missed by the entire town.

Alan Salter
Daughter of James Salter, beautiful intelligent, sensitive, a warm wonderful spirit still missed who was electrocuted in the shower of father's guest house due to faulty wiring.

Patty Green
Blonde Buxom good-natured waitress at the pub. OD on heroin.

Toby Grundeman
Cook at Mother Lode, landscaper. Big, affable guy, played on Pub softball team, "dad" of "Pancho" a Newfoundland mix town character dog. drug overdose/heart attack. Gentle easygoing person missed by all.

David Rosen
San Franciso transplant, short time Aspen resident. Started first espresso shop in town,

former US Ski Team Chile ski camp organizer. Accident while having seizure. Bright gentle person, liked and missed by those who knew him.

Michael Sutton

From Chicago, Owner of the Centre, then Little Nells. Quiet, nice person, got along with everyone, drug overdose. Missed.

Pam Craven

Very sweet, well liked lady, Colorado girl. Married to attorney Buzzy Ware. Killed at Shale Bluffs on the back of Harley (crash). Much loved and missed.

There are many omissions here, none by design, and all that have passed have our respect and gratitude.

Index

Buddy Ortega, 183
Buddha, 216
Budget, 267, 268
Buick, 248
Bumble Boogie, 16
Burky, 148
Burt, 82, 189, 190, 210
Buttermilk Mountain, 33,
50, 180
Buttermilk West, 251
Buzz Williams, 88
Buzzy Ware, 106

Cadillac, 140
California, 67, 158, 186, 233
Camels, 256
Canoga Park, Ca., 237
Carbondale, 31, 73, 143
Carl's Pharmacy, 34, 203
Castle Creek, 150
Capitol, 14
CC, 103, 104, 105, 106, 241
Central America, 43, 105
Centre, 68, 79, 80
Cervinia, 243, 276, 278
Cessna 172, 205
Chamonix, Fra., 276, 279
Charles, 166
Chicago, 5, 7, 11, 12, 13, 18,
22, 23, 24, 26, 27, 33, 57,
61, 67, 68, 69, 76, 82, 87,
125, 143, 149, 166, 169,
170, 171, 175, 177, 189,
191, 202, 233, 260, 261, 263
Chicago Heights, 169
Chile, 250, 258
Chuck and Joan, 63
Chuckles, 37
CIA, 139
Cincinnati, 256

Citations, 205
Claudine, 271, 272
Colorado, 26, 34, 48, 61, 82,
145, 166, 167, 222, 257,
261, 263, 287
Cold war, 66
Columbia, 14, 143, 144, 145,
146, 149, 151
Columbian Gold, Columbo,
143, 162, 163, 176,
229. 263, 287
Congress, 211
Continental Inn, 100
Connie, 170, 260
Connie Cohen, 169
Cooper Street Pier, 271
Cowboy Frank, 64, 65
Cowboy Mafia, 146
Conoco, 204
Crested Butte, 143, 144
Crystal River, 73
CTA, 12
Curtis Mayfield, 129, 197

Dallas/Fort Worth, 168
Danny, 149
Danny Wardwell, 34
Darrel, 163, 165
Darren, 63, 64
David Rosen, 250, 257
Dayton, Dayton, Ohio, 11,
17, 20, 189
DC, 5, 218
DC6, 145
DEA, 146, 211, 286
Delaware Towers, 15
Delta, 244
Democratic Convention, 5,
22, 27
Donny the Coach, 161,
162, 163

Harriet Garth, 115
Harvey Rose, 128
Hawaii, 255, 260
Hawaiian, 125, 127, 274, 276
Hector, 150
Hedford, 70, 103, 161
Heinz Grist, 159, 160
Henry Betts, 160, 161
Henry Hooks, 160
Hells' Angels, 139
Highlands, 80, 94
Highway Patrol, 45, 99, 164
Hippie Mafia, 146
Hollywood, 205
Hong Kong, 210
Hopkins St., 113, 158, 191
Hotel Jerome, 32, 34, 79, 204
Hotel Sapinerre, 279
House of Lum, 125, 127
Hunter Thompson, 161
Hyatt Intercontinental, 210

Illinois, 48
Indian, 48, 237, 238, 240
Indonesia, 210, 212
Instant Karma, 7
Irish, 132
Italian, 273
Italy, 276

Jack Kerouac, 7
Jack Nicholson, 180
Jaime Menos, 149, 153
Jakarta, 212
Japan, 210
Jeep, 45
Jeff McAllister, 115
Jerome B. Wheeler Public
House, 95, 119

Jerry, 209, 221, 241,
281, 282
Jesse Madalone, 204
Jill St. John, 246
Jimi Hendrix, 139
Jim Less, 148
Jimmy Hoffa, 139
Joe Poleski, 64, 68, 70
Jim Weaks, 159, 160
Jockey Club, 166, 167
Joe, Joe Goldmann 233, 234,
235, 238, 240, 246, 248,
249, 250, 253, 260, 261
Joe Walsh, 21
John Denver, 250
John Dutton, 68, 69, 198
Jolly Hotel, 275
Jones, 158
Judge Shaw, 180

Kaiulani, 125, 127
Kansas, 145
Karl, 35, 36
Katie Price, 161
Kendall, 38, 39, 96, 119
Kennedy, 27
Kennedy Airport, 280
Keno, 184
Kent, 19, 21, 26
Kent State, 5, 7, 17, 110,
139
Kilometro Lanziatto, KL, 243
King Ranch, 67, 69
King St., 131
Kiwanis Club, 16
Kool-Aid, 134
Kyoto, 212

The Temptations, 139
The Who, 13, 14
Therese Donald, 113
Tim Chaz, 160, 161
Tim Leary, 7
Tina Rubey, 115
Tina Turner, 139
Titanic, 23
Tokyo, 210, 212, 218
Tommy Lee, 222, 228
Tommy Simons, 241, 242, 244, 245, 247, 253, 258, 272, 279
Tower Road, 267
Tragedy Manor, 96
Tucson, 81, 82
Tugboat, 119
Two o'clock Shuffle, 71
Twelve stepping, 6

U-Haul, 27, 31
Undiscovered Aspen, 8
US Ski Team, 241, 254
Ute Indians, 75

Valhalla, 190
Van Morrison, 129, 197
Vegas, 250, 271, 281
Velvet Underground, 13
Vickie, 248
Viet Nam, 5, 24, 130, 139
Vitamin C, 15
Volvo, 191, 193

Wagner Park, 158
Warhol, 14
Warner's, 14
Washington, 210, 218

W. C. Fields, 66, 166
Werner Erhart, 132
Wheeler Opera House, 95
White, 40, 43, 44, 45, 48, 49, 55
White Horse Springs, 126
Wilson Pickett, 139
Wingbat, 140, 141, 157
Wellesley, 83
Wooden Handle, 56, 61, 77, 192
Woody Creek, 121, 126
Wolf, 238
World Cup, 253
World Pro Skiing, 104
Wurlitzer, 18

Your Father's Mustache, 25